SOUTH ASIAN RESPONSES TO CHINUA ACHEBE

In the Same Series

The Novels of Wole Soyinka
M. Rajeshwar

Indian Response to African Literature
Ed. A Ramakrishna Rao and C.R. Visweswara Rao

Recent Commonwealth Literature (2 vols.)
Ed. R.K. Dhawan, P.V. Dhamija, A.K. Shrivastava

Australian Literature and Indian Literature: Studies in Mutual Response
Ed. David Kerr and R.K. Dhawan

Australian Literature Today
Ed. R.K. Dhawan and David Kerr

New Zealand Literature Today
Ed. R.K.Dhawan and Walter Tonetto

A.D. Hope: Questions of Poetic Strength
Walter Tonetto

The Novels of V.S. Naipaul
Shashi Kamra

SOUTH ASIAN RESPONSES

TO

CHINUA ACHEBE

Edited by
Bernth Lindfors
Bala Kothandaraman

PRESTIGE

Published by
Prestige Books International
New Delhi 110 060

ISBN 81-85218-66-8

Phototypesetting by
data culture
New Delhi 110 065
Ph. 6431070

Printed at
Mehra Offset Press
New Delhi 110 002

CONTENTS

PREFACE

This book, a collection of specially written essays, is intended both as a tribute to Chinua Achebe and as an appreciation of his works. No other African writer has reached readers in so many parts of the world and won such an enthusiastic following; no other has produced literature that has sold so well at home and abroad. His novels, essays and poems have been hailed as contemporary classics and are now being studied intensively in schools and universities all over the globe. As a consequence, he has transcended his local environment and become an international literary phenomenon. He is still a native son, but he also belongs to a larger community, especially to that family of nations that have undergone colonial and postcolonial transformation. Today Achebe's art speaks not only to and for Africa but also to and for much of the rest of the "Third World," not least through its successful challenge of "First World" centricity.

It is therefore interesting to observe how readers situated in the wider world react to his writing. Some who live and work in circumstances similar to those described in his books may experience a genuine shock of recognition. Others may be intrigued by settings, characters and actions that they find odd or inexplicable. Those interested primarily in politics may search for overt and covert ideological statements, and those fascinated by language may carefully scrutinize aspects of Achebe's innovative style. Comparisons will abound, for readers moving from one tradition of verbal art to another will naturally set the two traditions side by side, if only to clarify salient points of similarity and difference. Indeed, all critics who view Achebe's work from an alien (i.e., nonindigenous—in this case, non-Igbo) perspective will have to establish some common ground or at least devise a stable, consistent frame of reference that, buttressed by frequent recourse to the text in hand, will enable them to some extent to cross borders and enter more fully into a universe of discourse that they do not ordinarily inhabit. Ultimately, they must become informed interlopers, instructed in how to read and interpret local signs as distinguished from, or in addition to, their common grounding in the Eng. Lit. tradition.

Such expert navigational tendencies are evident in the essays collected here, all but one of which have been written by South Asian scholars who teach or study African literature. Since these explorers live in different parts of the world (India, Sri Lanka, Bahrain, Singapore, Australia, Canada, England, and the United States of America) and were trained in a variety of educational institutions, their approaches to Achebe cover a pluralistic range. Several of them have worked or travelled extensively in Africa; some have written a great deal on African, Indian and other so-called "New Literatures in English"; and a few are young scholars making their first entry into print. Yet all share a deep appreciation of Achebe's writing, recognizing that it is in literature of such striking originality, beauty and force that the potential for meaningful cross-cultural communication can be realized. Achebe is the consummate translator of African culture, and this quality makes his work as relevant and important in South Asia as it is throughout the African continent.

Crossing Over

(for Achebe on his 60th)

KIRPAL SINGH

believe me brother, believe me
i tried to tell them, my brothers,
how things fell apart like the way you said,
i tried to tell them in the wet season and the dry,
i said, look here, learn from the spider's web,
learn, there's morning yet on creation day.

alas, here there is no man of the people
the kiasus rule the day, the times, the morals,
hearts of darkness, feet of clay, minds for money,
oh how can i say what i really do want to say!

you taught me things, brother,
things my grandmother knew if i had listened—
i had to read fearfully at first, afraid
they'd find out, prevent this identification,
hinder the process of affinity,
move from the centre to the periphery.

now, no longer at ease, i have learnt
beware soul brother, the cunning's deep
dry mouths cannot grasp watery truths
nor spill the secrets of our prison.

my pride is wounded, my manhood suffers,
loss of my blood, loss of my elders,
my language breaks as hearts track feelings
across the savannah of my dreams.
here discoveries lie concealed, set us back,
betrayals gather momentum, spend our muscle.

someday the arrow of god will arrive
awaken in pain the waste of years, wasted youth,
uncover the knowledge of slavery, gift of freedom,
and the sun will bless the moonlit night.

Articulating the Postcolonial Writer's Social Responsibilities: The Example of Chinua Achebe

ANURADHA DINGWANEY NEEDHAM

A writer has the same kind of responsibility in all cultures, but the various elements of that responsibility come in different proportions according to the health of the community he's trying to serve. It is determined by historical predicament. In Nigeria there's a sense of the loss of initiative in your own history, the loss of responsibility. . . . And, of course, the view of the government as alien: in our traditional culture everybody was supposed to participate in the government. . . . Now, all that has gone. Within one generation people lose even the memory of what used to be.

The writer has a responsibility to remember what it was like before, and to keep talking about it. (Chinua Achebe in an interview with Jim Davidson 43).

I think they were books that had to be written. I see myself in historical terms as coming into being at a time when these books just had to be written. . . . Because, you see, there was a crisis . . . and [the crisis had] to be resolved. . . . It was a historic need.

> *We [i.e., the writers] were fulfilling our role in history.*
>
> (Chinua Achebe in an interview with Chinweizu 28-29).

> *But even in fighting revolutions, the particular place where you are fighting your particular revolution is going to a large extent to determine tactics.*
>
> (Chinua Achebe in interview with Ernest and Pat Emenyonu 25).

The vocabulary of accountability (words like "responsibility," "duty," "leadership") so permeates Chinua Achebe's many and varied discussions of a writer's role in society ("The Novelist as Teacher," "The Role of the Writer in a New Nation," "The Black Writer's Burden," to name a few) that it seems peculiarly redundant to even mention Achebe's articulations of the postcolonial writer's social responsibilities, much less make them the subject of an entire essay, as I propose to do. Yet, what Ketu H. Katrak calls "several disconcerting trends in the recent production and consumption of postcolonial theory" (158) make a detailed analysis of Achebe's conceptions of a writer's role in society peculiarly apt, even urgent, at this juncture. Among the trends Katrak isolates in her trenchant critique, she mentions especially that: 1) "little theoretical production of postcolonial writers [is] given the serious attention it deserves, or that it is dismissed as not theoretical enough, by Western Standards"; 2) there is "the increasing phenomenon of using postcolonial texts as raw material for theory producers and consumers of Western academia"; and 3) there is the impulse to treat "theoretical production as an end in itself, confined to the consumption of other theorists who speak the same privileged language in which obscurity is regularly mistaken for profundity." (158) Katrak's discomfiture at these trends arises from contemporary (poststructuralist) theorists' use of postcolonial texts for their own (Eurocentric) formulations and agendas at the same time as they elide or displace postcolonial texts from their historical, political, and cultural specificities and functions. An analysis of Achebe's theoretical pronouncements on the writer's social responsibilities—pronouncements, I would argue, that are deeply implicated with, indeed, integrally related to his fictional or imaginative works—allows us to both counter these trends and reclaim theory as a mode of *praxis*, a mode of resistance, and an aid to social transformation.

In this essay, then, I will examine Achebe's theoretical formulations in a variety of essays and interviews he has written/given over the past three decades, both insofar as they stake out the writer's role in society, and as they illuminate or comment upon the purpose and significance of his imaginative output. Before I begin, however, I should make it clear that, in general, for Achebe, the writer is, or can be, an initiator and agent of social transformation; in this, he[1] is both someone especially gifted—a leader and teacher of people—and empowered to show his people the way to a better, more promising future. Equally, however, the writer is a product of his historical moment, and, thus, fulfills an "historic need," in which case the power he wields is a function of that moment ("I see myself in historical terms as coming into being when these books just had to be written, and if I hadn't written them someone else would have done so"; in interview with Chinweizu 28-29).

* * *

> *[The prime duty of the African writer is to show his own community] that African people did not hear of culture for the first time from Europeans; that their societies were not mindless but frequently had a philosophy of great depth and value and beauty, that they had poetry, and, above all, they had dignity. It is this dignity that many African people all but lost during the colonial period and it is this that they must now regain. The worst thing that can happen to*

> *any people is the loss of their dignity and self-respect. The writer's duty is to help them regain it by showing them in human terms what happened to them, what they lost* (Achebe, "The Role of the Writer in a New Nation" 8).

Achebe's works—fictional and non-fictional—follow what Timothy Brennan calls "the rhythms of the decolonization process" (Brennan 80). Critical analyses of these works often refer to this fact. For instance, discussing the first phase, as it were, of the decolonization process—the physical and mental battle for political liberation from colonizers—Abdul JanMohamed notes: "While Chinua Achebe . . . [was] publishing [his] novels . . . *Things Fall Apart* . . . in 1958, *No Longer at Ease* in 1960 and *Arrow of God* in 1964 . . . Africa was being politically transformed." (11) As a *writer,* Achebe participated in this political transformation by intervening in and contesting the hegemonic misrepresentations of Africa in colonial/imperial discourses, and by setting up alternative "images" of Africa.

In essays that span the decade which follows the publication of his three early novels (1965-75), Achebe focuses on specific instances of the impact—and psychic costs—of colonial values and rhetoric on the excolonized peoples and cultures of Africa. In "The Novelist as Teacher," for example, he refers to "the shock felt by Christians of my father's generation in my village in the forties when, for the first time, the local girls' school performed Nigerian dances at the anniversary of the coming of the gospel," whereas earlier "they had always put on . . . the Maypole dance" (*Morning* 44). One of the major points of this essay, however, is to underscore the continuing, debilitating existence of colonial values and rhetoric in post-independence Nigeria where students regard the use of a word like *harmattan* as "bush" and find "the palm-tree" an unfit "subject for poetry" (44). What is at issue, of course, is the denigration of culturally specific words and the "reality" or "experience" to which they refer. For, as Frantz Fanon has observed: "To speak a language is to take on a world, a culture" (*Black Skins, White Masks* 38); by the same token, to *refuse* to speak a language is to deny (and thereby denigrate) the culture that language points to. This refusal issues, in terms of Achebe's argument, from the persistence of colonial values and discourse and alienation from a people's own values and culture. Hence, Achebe sees his task as a writer mapped out: "Here then is an adequate revolution for me to espouse—to help my society regain belief in itself and put away the complexes of the years of denigration and self-abasement. And it is essentially a question of education, in the best sense of that word" (*Morning* 44).

Since his society's "denigration and self-abasement" arise from the impact of Africa's "first confrontation with Europe" (44) and are a product primarily of colonialist misrepresentations of Africa, Achebe intervenes to expose their racist underpinnings and hegemonic functions. He further delimits his task by taking on two writers, Joyce Cary and Joseph Conrad, and their representations of Africa.

About Cary, Achebe's comments are succinct. In his essay, "Africa and Her Writers," while discussing Ayi Kwei Armah's "scornful, cold, and remote . . . obsession with the filth of Ghana," Achebe notes, "you have to go to the early European writres on Africa to find something of the same attitude and icy distance"; this comment precedes a paragraph-long quote from Cary's description of Fada in *Mister Johnson* (*Morning* 26). More significantly, in an interview with Lewis Nkosi, Achebe remarks: "Joyce Cary's novel set in Nigeria, *Mister Johnson*, . . . was praised so much, and it was clear to me that this was a most superficial picture. . . . So I thought . . . Someone ought to try and look at this from the inside" (Pictcrsc and Ducrdcn 4). The brevity of these comments should not belie the significance of Achebe's choice of *Mister Johnson* as a work he must counter. First, as Achebe himself notes, "It was praised so much." Second, Oladele Taiwo observes, *Mister Johnson* "is widely read in Nigeria and has often been set for public examinations." (18) Thus, its representations of Nigeria enjoy currency there and "the African image in these novels might have influenced the Nigerian writer's consciousness a great deal" (Taiwo 18). Finally, and most importantly, Taiwo notes, "Cary *writes as one* who knows Africa well and is deeply committed to its development," that is, he writes as someone who claims to know Nigeria from *inside* (13; 22; emphases added). Thus, Cary's "success" among Nigerians is due to his presumed intimacy with his subject matter and also due to his assignment of active and important roles to Africans. Why does Achebe take issue with him? Although Cary's treatment of Nigeria is seen as sympathetic, he nevertheless relies on the familiar analytic categories of colonial discourse whereby the Nigerians are characterized as "savages," "barbarians," "bush pagans" unaffected by the "battles of civilization"; furthermore, at a time (1936) when Nigerians were becoming conscious of their political rights and organizing around them, Cary completely ignored what Arnold Kettle calls "the rising tide of African national consciousness" (quoted in Taiwo 22-23). Thus Achebe's attempt to counter Cary's fictive representations underline not only the fact that he has cut through their liberal facade, but also that Cary's apparently sympathetic representations of Nigerians are insidious and more dangerous because they might preempt a serious critique of Cary's reliance on colonial discourses about Africa.

Against Conrad, Achebe is far more detailed and polemical. In "An Image of Africa," Achebe calls Conrad "a bloody racist," (788) who "chose the role of purveyor of comforting myths" (784). The Conradian world Achebe describes is one built on Manichean dualism: "*Heart of Darkness* projects the image of Africa as 'the other world,' the antithesis of Europe and therefore of civilization, a place where man's vaunted intelligence and refinement are finally mocked by triumphant bestiality" (783); Africa is a "place of negations," Europe a place (and state) of "spiritual grace" (783). Of course since Achebe's essay was published, critics like Edward Said have argued for a more complicated and complex position on the part of Conrad; nevertheless, Said's analysis concurs with Achebe's fundamental assertions (see especially, "Intellectuals in the Post-Colonial World" 48-49; 52).[2] By now, of course, Achebe's essay has itself acquired a sort of canonical status among postcolonial writers and critics; thus, it is difficult to assess the novelty of its position or its impact on his first listeners/readers.[3] But appearing as it did in 1975/77, it stakes out a reading that was among the first to locate *Heart of Darkness* politically and examine it as an instance—a brilliant instance to be sure—of an essentially colonial view of Africa.

So far I have focused on the "content" of Achebe's remarks that seek to restore dignity to his people by exposing Cary's and Conrad's misrepresentations of Africa and its cultures. It is valuable, in addition, in tracking Achebe's articulation of a postcolonial writer's responsibilities, to reflect on his strategy—how he says what he says and why. Cary's *Mister Johnson* is treated with brevity and in occasional remarks made in the course of an interview and an essay. *Heart of Darkness*, on the other hand, is analyzed in a detailed and polemical argument supported by textual evidence and tied carefully into certain categories of colonial discourses about Africa. Why? Because Cary's work does not have the same canonical status that *Heart of Darkness* still enjoys as one of the "masterpieces" of English literature. If readers, who have a great emotional and intellectual investment in *Heart of Darkness*, are to be provoked into "rethinking" their views, Achebe must give the work the extended treatment that in fact he does. The differential space(s) allotted to Cary and Conrad bear out that Achebe is conscious as well that an effort that aims to bring about (social) transformation must adopt tactics that bear directly on particular efforts, or the forum in which you choose to carry out your revolution, to adapt a comment from Achebe, will "to a large extent . . . determine tactics" (Emenyonu and Emenyonu 25).

Achebe does not castigate European writers alone for their failure to represent Africa accurately. He also takes to task fellow African writers, scholars and critics like Yambo Ouologuem, Ayi Kwei Armah and Sunday Anozie for succumbing to colonial representations of Africa and its peoples. Thus Ouologuem's *Bound to Violence* is critiqued for recycling an essentially colonial image of Africans when he invests them "with responsibility for violence and evil" (*Morning* 10); Armah is described as an "alienated native," who "imposes so much foreign metaphor on the sickness of Ghana that it ceases to be true" (*Morning* 26); and Anozie is seen as a misdirected critic and scholar, who aspires to Eurocentric standards of "universality," and hence ends up negating the political and socially responsible fictions of African writers like Christopher Okigbo (*Morning* 13-14).

The terms of Achebe's critique of Ouologuem, Armah, and Anozie are firmly bolted into his overarching concern with those functions of art and culture that can help his people regain their dignity and trust in themselves as finally arbiters of their own destiny. In this regard, therefore, it is important to bear in mind that Achebe's critical assessment of these three African writers is not premised on a monolithic denunciation of the West. Instead, what troubles him is how, in order to "win applause in Western circles" (*Morning* 27) these writers, though possessing "enormous talents and energy" (*Morning* 25) use their talents in the service of recycling what are essentially colonial myths underwriting Europe's and the West's power; and this at a time when the West continues to wield enormous political and cultural power over the non-Western world: "In talking about the world here we really mean Europe and the West" (*Morning* 24). In such a situation—where critics like Anozie decry African writers' presumption to be agents of social change (*Morning* 13) and writers like Armah and Ouologuem deny their specificities as African writers (*Morning* 26-27) or represent Africa as inherently violent and evil (*Morning* 9-11)—these writers do irreparable harm to what should ideally be the primary concern of African writers: to restore dignity to their peoples. In such a situation, therefore, it becomes imperative for Achebe to determine "just on whose ideological side they are playing" (*Morn-*

ing 12).

* * *

> *It suddenly seemed that we too might have a story to tell* (Achebe, quoted in David Carroll 13).

Just how does the African writer go about the business of reclaiming African history form the hands of the colonizers? First, as I have argued above, he exposes the false or inadequate accounts of African cultures and peoples by European and African writers. Second, he provides alternative accounts of his culture and people. (Of course, as Achebe's example bears out, the two tasks are not carried out sequentially but simultaneously.)

Things Fall Apart offers one such alternative account.[4] Although virtually all of Achebe's novels can be understood, at least in part, "as analyses and products of the historical problems created by colonization" (Jan Mohamed 183), *Things Fall Apart*, published before Nigeria achieved independence and set in the latter part of the nineteenth century, deals with the coming of the English and of English political control; it presents Igbo society both *before* (i.e., in pre-colonial times) and *after* colonization, and examines the steady erosion and overwhelming of Igbo culture so that, by the end, things have literally fallen apart. Critics have noted that the book is Achebe's attempt to counter some of the egregious misrepresentations of Africa by Europeans (Africans had no history, no culture till the Europeans came to redeem them; Africans were/are savages—mute, passive, irrational). Set against a "background of details of Igbo village life," *Things Fall Apart* presents "a well-ordered society in which individual achievement is honored, hard work is expected, close ties are maintained to ancestors and spirits, government is a form of participatory democracy" (Schleh 128). This book is a sympathetic insider's account of the inner workings of Igbo society, its complex springs of actions and motivations. What is particularly distinctive about *Things Fall Apart* is that Achebe is not interested simply in what Edward Said, in a different context, has called a "politics of blame" ("Intellectuals in the Post-Colonial World," 46). The culture and society of Umuofia break down under pressure from both within and without. This is not to suggest that these pressures are examined and evaluated in the same way. But, it seems to me that Achebe is more interested in probing and opening up for inspection the processes that lead to the disintegration of this society, in exploring, to adapt one of Achebe's favourite proverbs, when (and why) the rain began to beat upon them. Thus, his analysis proceeds from a detailed, loving, but not idyllic, account of a hierarchical, gendered society where power rests in male hands; it is also a society that kills twins because they are considered aberrant, not "natural" or "human," and excludes the *osu* as despised outcasts.[5] At the center of Achebe's narrative is the protagonist, Okonkwo, a man of "inflexible will," (21) who tells his children "masculine stories of violence and bloodshed," and whose definition of what constitutes manhood is crucially tied to controlling "his women and his children (and especially his women)" (46). To this society the English missionaries bring the promise of a "true" God and bicycles technology (130). Achebe's description of the onslaught of colonialism aptly focuses on the violence of the colonial encounter and the colonizer's duplicity:

> The white man is very clever. He came quietly and peaceably with his religion. We were amused at his foolishness and allowed him to stay. Now he has won our brothers, and our clan can no longer act like one. He has put a knife on the things that held us together and we have fallen apart. (158)

Thus, the colonizers succeed *both* because of their duplicity and their willingness to use brute physical force *and* because the disenfranchised of the indigenous society, having been denied a place in their society, become their willing converts. On balance, however, the inner contradictions and problems of Umuofia society (of which Okonkwo is simultaneously an extreme emblem and, in his extreme position, somewhat the exception) are judged less harshly than the colonizers' brutal intervention in this society. And though the last words of the novel—the title of a book—belong to the colonial Commissioner (a sign that colonialism has come to stay), they are chilling, heavily ironized words, incorporating as they do a familiar colonial stereotype of the African "primitives" vs. the "enlightened" English: *The Pacification of the Primitive Tribes of the Lower Niger.*

The difficulties in striking a clear balance in parcelling out *responsibility* for the disintegration of Umuofia are an index of the treacherous discursive terrain Achebe must negotiate. In a 1972 interview with Ernest and Pat Emenyonu, Achebe points out:

> There were certainly faults in the Igbo system that was depicted in *Things Fall Apart.* There is no reason, for instance, for twins to be thrown away. But if you take a position for or against, then you find yourself defending the throwing away of twins, or else you say that Africa is barbarism, which appears to be the new trend today among some black writers, and they are immediately applauded by whites because it gives them an easy conscience again after all this period of doubt (23).

Achebe's comments get to the heart of the problems the African writer faces while attempting to restore dignity and self-respect to his peoples. To invest them with their full humanity, he must present them as complex beings, capable of good and bad, capable of making mistakes, possessing both strength and weaknesses. Yet the writer must carry out this task in full awareness of the fact that his people's fallibilities can be and (wilfully) are re-appropriated under the familiar colonial/Western conceptualization of everything African as "primitive" or "barbaric."[6] Thus, while arguing for his peoples's humanity, he must resist as well such attempts at renewed cultural imperialism. In his sympathetic, but realistic, representation of Igbo culture, Achebe negotiates these problems carefully and responsibly.

* * *

> . . . the great collusive swindle that was independence (Achebe, quoted in Carroll 27).

In his 1972 interviews with Ernest and Pat Emenyonu, Achebe accounts for the shift in emphasis from his three early works, *Things Fall Apart*, *No Longer at Ease*, and *Arrow of God*, by remarking that "the post-independence period in Africa is bound to create in the writer a new approach. . . . The disenchantment with the fruits of independence was already there in the early sixties. *A Man of the People*, which came out in January 1966 and which I wrote in 1964 and 1965, shows quite clearly this new preoccupation with the reality of post-independent Africa." (25) The shift in emphasis produces also a shift in what Achebe sees as his responsibilities as a writer. His attention is now fixed solidly on the indigenous ruling elite, the Nangas and Sams and their acquiescent, grovelling henchmen, whose only ambition, after independence, seems to be to move into the spaces vacated by the colonizers, without reconstructing the political, social, and cultural arrangements left behind by the colonizers. Consider, for example, Ngugi's particularly acute account in "Towards a National Culture" of the motivations that drive the native ruling elite—an account that is also of a piece with Achebe's assessment of the post-independence rulers of Nigeria in *A Man of the People* and *Anthills of the Savannah:*

> In fighting for independence, some of the African intelligentsia only wanted that which was forbidden to them, or rather they saw the struggle in terms of their immediate needs, nurtured by the social position they had attained under the colonial system,

> whose fulfilment was however frustrated by the racism inherent in the system. . . . After independence, the racial barrier to their needs was broken. The gold-rush for the style of living of their former conquerors had started (*Homecoming* 12).

In *A Man of the People*, Odili, the narrator, draws our attention to Minister of Culture Nanga's "princely seven bathroom mansion with its seven gleaming, silent action, water closets!" while the rest of his countrymen must settle for squalid and unsanitary bucket and pit latrines— "The surprises and contrasts in our great country were simply inexhaustible" (46). And though Nanga dons the mantle of nationalism and adopts its rhetoric to acquire power and his position as Minister of Culture (6-7), his real power and wealth are underwritten by British Amalgamated. Similarly, Sam ("His Excellency" of *Anthills*) "imitat[es] the English" (51); "his major flaw," according to him, is "that all he ever wanted was to do what was expected of him especially by the English whom he admired sometimes to the point of foolishness" (49); and he preserves their rituals, the "sophisticated" cocktail/dinner party, held in the Presidential Retreat, "perch[ed] like a lighthouse," above and away, much like the colonizer's living spaces, from the living spaces of "the very people who legitimize [his] authority" (71-81).

One of the insights that lies at the heart of Achebe's novel set in preindependence Nigeria, *No Longer at Ease*, is that "In Nigeria, the government was 'they.' It had nothing to do with you or me. It was an alien institution and people's business was to get as much from it as they could without getting into trouble" (3). This insight explains, though it does not exonerate, the bribery and corruption described in this work. One would imagine that things would be different once the colonizers departed. Not so. Having simply moved into the vacuum created by the departing colonizers, without recreating society to serve the needs of its people, the ruling elite's corruption matches that of the colonial regime. The only difference is that the ruling elite must now be held accountable. Thus, a comparable insight, expressed somewhat differently, informs *A Man of the People.* As Robert Wren points out: "Not taking so much that the owner will notice is part of the novel's central theme. . . . What troubles Odili at the end is that in the new society there is no longer an 'owner' to notice" (109). Certainly the masses are cynical about "the great collusive swindle that was independence" (Achebe, quoted in Carroll 27) and fail to condemn the leaders who openly loot their nation's treasury. The world they inhabit has to do with what each of them can (or hope to) get of "the national cake":

> "Let them eat," was the people's opinion, "after all when white men used to do all the eating did we commit suicide?" Of course not. And where is the all-powerful white man today? He came, he ate and he went. But we are still around. The important thing then is to stay alive. . . . Besides, if you survive, who knows? it may be your turn to eat tomorrow. Your son may bring home your share. (161-62)

Achebe obviously does not share the cynicism of the masses. For him, there must always be an owner, for ownership implies being accountable to something (to his fledgling nation) and to someone (to his people); it implies taking on responsibility.[7] Accountability or taking on responsibility, in *A Man of the People,* takes on the form of an exposé—an exposé meant to warn his people about where they are headed. Thus. what seems like a bleak and pessimistic vision of postcolonial Nigeria is not entirely so, for Achebe is eager to point out that the situation is not hopeless:

> If you were convinced that it was absolutely hopeless, then you would just drink and wait for your death. But the fact that you are talking about it implies some optimism that somebody may listen,

> that there is still a possibility for change. . . .
>
> So one has to bring these problems out as forcefully as possible to draw attention to them. It has always been the method of teachers at all times. (Emenyonu and Emenyonu 25)

* * *

> Writers in the Third World context must not stop at the stage of documenting social problems but move to the higher responsibility of proffering prescription. . . .
>
> "Writers don't give prescriptions," shouted Ikem. "*They give headaches*!" (*Anthills of the Savannah* 148)

Written after a long break from fiction-writing—a break during which Achebe eschewed the novel because it "is a slow and rather luxurious form of statement," and settled, instead, for more "direct statement" in essays (Moss 1677)—*Anthills of the Savannah* marks a distinctive, more contemporary, moment in Achebe's reflections on the writer's role(s) in society. Despite Ikem's contention that writers don't prescribe, "they give headaches!" *Anthills*, unlike *A Man of the People,* is not just an exposé of what his young nation has become and of the people who are responsible for the tragic state of affairs, but also is informed by a "higher responsibility" whereby Achebe points towards a solution—a tentative blueprint of what must be done—and, more importantly, identifies who will do it. To an extent, then, *Anthills* both offers a critique and shows the way to remoulding society.[8]

At least as early as 1972, Achebe had begun to reflect on who would bring about the necessary transformation so that postcolonial Nigerian society could be regenerated. Not surprisingly, his reflections depend upon what has so far gone wrong, from what source regeneration could not arise: "The masses have not changed," according to Achebe, "the masses would still be as cynical, which is not to say that they should therefore be abandoned to their lot. . . . But that does not absolve the leaders." In fact, for Achebe,

> The whole point of being a leader is that, in spite of the cynicism or the despair of the masses, it is [the leader's] job to do something for them. [The masses] don't have to deserve it because they are law-abiding, sensible and obedient. After all, whether they are or not, they are still brothers, sisters, fathers and mothers (Emenyonu and Emenyonu 27).

This is a pretty stringent, almost ascetic conceptualization of what a leader should be—someone who performs his tasks despite what the masses do, without expecting rewards or even encouragement. Further, it is a view of leadership that eschews any view of change or social transformation proceeding from grass roots activism. Here the initiative definitely rests with the leaders, and flows from the top down.

In a more recent interview (1987) conducted by Anna Rutherford soon after *Anthills* was nominated for the Booker Prize, Achebe concurs with Rutherford's suggestion that *Anthills* is about "issues of leadership," specifically about who has the "ultimate responsibility for getting us [i.e. Nigerians] out of this bad patch." The burden, for Achebe, rests with "the small group of people who, in one way or another, find themselves in positions of leadership. They have a special responsibility" (2). Interestingly, he identifies Ikem, the editor of the *National Gazette*, as one such leader who "initiate[s] the action" to "correct the situation" (2). Ikem's principal method of correction is the exposé: "crusading editorials," "essays in overkill" that, in Chris's judgment are "futile" and "counterproductive" because they "antagonize everybody" (*Anthills* 38). Obviously Ikem thinks otherwise: "But the real irony of the situation is that my own method is more successful even on Chris's own terms"

(*Anthills* 46). Ikem proceeds on the belief that he can bring about change. And he does; his death and Chris's death serve as the catalyst that brings "a group," a "small company around Beatrice" together, which, thereafter, presages "the possibility of a new beginning. A new dispensation. . ." (Rutherford 3). But even before his death Ikem has initiated change, indeed provoked it through his incendiary rhetoric and passion. In fact, it is because he poses a threat to the ruling elite that he is fired from his job and then arrested and murdered. For Achebe change is as much a function of a genuine leader as it is of the historical moment, but the leader is critical for success:

> But if you look really seriously at revolutions, you will see that the great changes in history have been brought about by a handful of people. It is true also that you might say 'The times were ripe.' And no one can dispute that either; the two must play a part. But I think the spark, this little catalyst without which a chemical change will not happen, is vital. This critical element has to be brought in before you can energize the mixture into action. And this is the role of this leadership: to create the circumstance in which the people begin to act with awareness (Rutherford 3).

It is hard not to see Ikem as a stand-in for Achebe and his views about the role of leadership, a role which in the interview and in *Anthills* is conflated with that of the critical writer. It is not a coincidence, for example, that Achebe's own method of education and correction so far has been to *expose* the chicaneries of colonial administrators and functionaries and the indigenous ruling elite, as too his earlier essays expose European and some African writers' reliance on colonial/Western misrepresentation of Africa.

It is not surprising, then, that the elder statesman of the delegation from Abazon—the delegation whose arrival in Bassa brings to a head the crisis in the government and, in a sense, forces the transformation of society to begin—assigns the story teller (and writer) the most significant role as agent of social transformation. Furthermore, the elder's oration about the role of the writer resonates richly with a vocabulary we have encountered before in Achebe:

> To some of us the Owner of the World has apportioned the gift to tell their fellows that the time to get up has finally come. To others He gives the eagerness to rise when they hear the call . . . to engage the invading enemy boldly in battle. And there are those others whose part is to wait and when the struggle is ended, to take over and recount its story . . . each is important in its own way. . . . But if you ask me which of them takes the eagle-feather I will say boldly: the story [and, hence, the storyteller].
>
> So why do I say that the story is chief among his fellows? . . . Because it is only the story . . . that outlives the sound of the war-drums and the exploits of brave fighters. It is the story, not the others, that saves our progeny from blundering like blind beggars. . . . The story is our escort; without it, we are blind (123-24).

Achebe is far more explicit in his privileging of the writer in his interview with Rutherford. To Rutherford's comment "Whilst this book is obviously about leadership, it is also very clearly about the art of story-telling," Achebe responds:

> Yes, the very nature of the story is one of the key issues in this novel. . . . How does the role of the story as the escort of the people compare with other factors in their lives? You have the story, you have the story-teller . . . and the way in which those who commandeer power would wish to commandeer his-

> tory and so would be afraid of story-tellers. Stories are not harmless, they are not innocent. The budding dictator would be afraid and quite anxious about the story and the story-teller and the story-teller could be in deep trouble in such a situation (5).[9]

With *Anthills* we seem to have come full circle in Achebe's articulation of the postcolonial writer's responsibility: his early essays and interviews ask/appeal to the African writer to take on the responsibility for transforming his society. And, to an extent, Achebe's fictions measure up to the responsibilities he maps out. In the elder's oration, the writer/story-teller as someone who transforms and leads his society is presented as an accomplished fact, as that which the writer inevitably delivers.

Before I conclude my discussion of *Anthills*, I should point out that in choosing Beatrice as the central presence around which others group together to bring about "a new dispensation," Achebe is adding on to what he conceives of as the writer's duty by taking into account the significance of women as agents of social transformation: "The position of Beatrice as sensitive leader of that group is indicative of what I see as necessary in the transition to the kind of society which I think we should be aiming to create." But, Achebe is also correct to include the disclaimer that "the woman herself will be in the forefront in designing what her new role is going to be" (Rutherford 4).[10]

* * *

Achebe's efforts to transform his society and culture are not limited to the discursive formulations in his fictional and nonfictional works. He has also been concerned with more pragmatic tasks that need to be addressed to develop an African literary tradition. Among these, I would note his contribution in setting up a literary magazine, *Okike*. For him a literary magazine "is a must" because "you cannot expect a magazine based in New York or London or Paris to [forward the cause(s) of your own culture] for you. They have their own business, their own people, their own culture to defend and project" (Chinweizu 26). He has also been enthusiastic in his support for creating "a book business" that has "an indigenous base" because, says Achebe,

> if we are going to grow at all, we won't grow by shuttling between Lagos and London, or Lagos and Paris and New York. I think London, Paris, and New York will, in future, come here and take what catches their fancy from what we produce. Like anybody else, they'll compete for what we have and reissue abroad works which originate with local publishers (Chinweizu 25).

At the same time as these statements address pragmatic concerns, the statements are also visionary and radical when we consider that most writers and critics from the "Third" world privilege publication houses and journals in the "First" world as the appropriate site and forum for their work. Often, then, they end up primarily addressing (or, at least, taking into account) readers located in the "First" world. In asserting that "an indigenous base" is not only appropriate, but also required for publishing and disseminating the work of African writers, Achebe is re-conceptualizing how these works should be presented and recuperated.

Achebe's many and diverse statements about what constitutes an African writer's responsibilities all refer back to one overarching purpose: the writer must restore dignity and self-respect to his people. Although Achebe's statements are anchored firmly in his concern for his own people, the means he suggests whereby a writer can restore confidence in his people are means that other postcolonial writers also incorporate in their works. These include: an effort to reclaim initiative in their own histories, rewrite and make themselves the subjects of their own histories, and write, as well, "alternative" histories ("alternative" histories for Achebe and other postcolonial writers involve rewriting both European misrepresentations of ex-colonized cultures and people and accounts circulated by the indigenous ruling elite to shore up their power. Often the project of writing "alternative" histories is conceived of as the task of memory against forgetting). Achebe's work, then, both contributes to and is part of the still-growing body of postcolonial writing; in this regard the significance of his work is not limited to African peoples alone.

NOTES

1. Achebe, without exception, uses the masculine pronoun and discusses, mostly, male writers in his essays.
2. See also the discussion that follows Said's essay and his contributions to that discussion (72-74); and see Peter Nazareth's essay in *Conradiana*, 14 (1982): 173-87.
3. First delivered as the second Chancellor's Lecture at University of Massachusetts, Amherst, on February 18, 1975; later published in *The Massachusetts Review* 18 (1977): 782-94.
4. Ama Ata Aidoo's comment on Achebe is particularly instructive in this regard:

> You come to literature or things like that, and it's then that you really understand a term like neocolonialism. . . . Because of the colonial experience we still, unfortunately, are very much lacking in confidence in ourselves and what belongs to us. . . . Until quite recently, we thought that a book was written by a white man.
>
> . . . this is the reason why I love Achebe: that, you know, he gave us so much—to me anyway he gave so much in confidence (Pieterse and Duerden 26).

5. Achebe's comments about reclaiming a precolonial past in "The Role of the Writer in a New Nation," are worth considering at

this point:

> The question is how does a writer re-create this past? Quite clearly there is a strong temptation to idealize it—to extol its good points and pretend that the bad never existed. . . .
>
> This is where the writer's integrity comes in. Will he be strong enough to overcome the temptation to select only those facts which flatter him? If he succumbs he will have branded himself as an untrustworthy witness. But it is not only his personal integrity as an artist which is involved. The credibility of the world he is attempting to recreate will be called to question and he will defeat his own purpose if he is suspected of glossing over inconvenient facts. We cannot pretend that our past was one long, technicolour idyll. We have to admit that like other people's pasts ours had its good as well as its bad sides (9).

6. Achebe takes issue with Ouologuem's *Bound to Violence* precisely because it re-inscribes a familiar colonial stereotype.

7. Consider, for example, Ngugi's astute assessment of *A Man of the People:*

> What Achebe has done in *A Man of the People* is to make it impossible or inexcusable for other African writers to do other than address themselves directly to their audiences in Africa—not in a comforting spirit—and tell them that such problems are their concern. The teacher no longer stands apart to contemplate. He has moved with a whip among the pupils, flagellating himself as well as them. He is now the true man of the people (*Homecoming* 54).

8. I am indebted, for part of my argument about *Anthills* to Leonard Podiṣ and Yakubu Saaka's unpublished essay, "Achebe's *Anthills of the Savannah* and Ngugi's *Petals of Blood:* The Creation of a Usable Past." I thank them both for allowing me to read and use it for my own analysis.

9. Here Achebe sounds uncannily like Salman Rushdie, who, in a 1983 interview with Rani Dharker, while discussing "the control of history by those who are powerful," says:

> It seems to me nowadays that it is very important for writers who can make alternate histories, who can put other pictures of the world to the ones the world would have you believe, to do that and to become adversaries of that process. And this is why politicians [Achebe's "budding dictator"], the more repressive politicians get more frightened of writers . . . because writers can threaten a view of the world that is false (360).

10. According to Podis and Saaka, "Such an approach to depicting women represents a new departure for Achebe" (21).

Ezeulu and Elesin: Faith and Change in Achebe's *Arrow of God* and Soyinka's *Death and the King's Horseman*

RADHAMANI GOPALAKRISHNAN

The fall of the two titanic figures Ezeulu and Elesin is the outcome of the clash between faith and change witnessed by Nigeria during the period of colonial administration. The specific geographical or ethnic identity serves only as a starting point, representing such experiences all over the world. Faith would not die; nor would it surrender to pressure even if it cracks under the impact. The irreversible law of change begins operating, crushing the individual in the process. Such situations of high tragic potential characterized by emotional intensity and historical authenticity reflect the spirit of Africa during the crucial phase of transition in the first decades of the twentieth century. Ezeulu in Chinua Achebe's novel *Arrow of God* and Elesin in Wole Soyinka's play *Death and the King's Horseman* are two giants whose collapse reverberates throughout the world. Friction between the emotional need to adhere to one's traditional faith and the practical compulsion to yield to the winds of change adds to the toll of victims during the ruthless march of history.

A comparison between the novel *Arrow of God* and the play *Death and the King's Horseman* involves cutting across two literary genres with very few points in common in details of craftsmanship. When history condenses itself into a situation or a moment of density, the vast canvas of a novel shrinks into an intensely lyrical context. This is the point at which novel, drama and lyric meet. History stretches itself across the pages of Achebe's novel with epic dimensions. In Soyinka's play, history crystallizes into a tense moment of unsurpassed tragic grandeur.

Death-pangs of Faith when it confronts Change find expression in both the works. History is based on the twin principles of challenge and response. The collapse in *Arrow of God* as well as the challenge in *Death and the King's Horseman* are true to the history of a people. The scope of a novel for working out themes differs from that of a play; yet both Ezeulu and Elesin stand together as symbols of resistance and defeat in a crucial period of social and spiritual crisis in Nigeria.

Achebe believes in the social function of literature and does not subscribe to the view that "pure" art should be uncommitted and remain aloof from society. Considering his own works as "applied art" (Emenyonu and Emenyonu 21-27), he asserts that literature "must, in other words, speak of a particular place, evolve out of the necessities of its history, past and current, and the aspirations and destinies of its people" (*Morning* 7).

Working out the intricate organic relationship between the individual and society at every phase of history, Achebe has explained that his specific purpose was to show that the African post "with all its imperfections—was not one long night of savagery from which the first Europeans acting on God's behalf delivered [Africans]" (*Morning* 45).

Explaining the role of a writer in the context of such tensions, Achebe specifies the nature of the fundamental theme in his novels:

> This theme—put quite simply—is that African people did not hear of culture for the first time from Europeans; that their societies were not mindless but frequently had a philosophy of great depth and value and beauty, that they had poetry, and, above all, they had dignity. It is this dignity that many African people all but lost during the colonial period and it is

> this that they must now regain. The worst thing that can happen to any people is the loss of their dignity and self-respect. The writer's duty is to help them regain it by showing them in human terms what happened to them, what they lost ("Role of the Writer" 12).

Soyinka's play *Death and the King's Horseman* echoes the same view through the words of Olunde, Elesin's son, a medical student in England. Olunde represents the new generation and is eager to stem the tide of the erosion of traditional values even at the cost of his own life. Olunde stands his ground with Mrs. Pilkings, wife of the District Officer:

> You [the English] believe that everything which appears to make sense was learnt from you (53).

On further arguments from her asserting the superiority of British education and culture as sources of enlightenment, he adds:

> You make it sound as if when I left, I took nothing at all with me (54).

Committing himself to recapitulating the historical process over a series of generations, Achebe presents his novels as authentic records of the ethnocentric history of Nigeria in general and of the Igbos in particular; in their scientific commitment to reality, these novels are anthropological.

Arthur Ravenscroft explains the theme of *Arrow of God:*

> The theme of the novel is a man's use of the power he already wields, his desire to extend it and the effects of his misuse of it upon himself and his people (Blamires 3).

This desire is the weakness which finally paves the way for the strong man's collapse and fall. Ezeulu's refusal to accept the pleas of his clan, and the insistence on having his own decision implemented even when he knew it was not the right one make him lose even the god's favour. As D.S. Izevbaye points out, "Ezeulu's *hubris* is his refusal to eat the new yam in spite of these precedents" and "his determination to avenge his wronged god blinds him to the established adaptive processes of his society" (144).

Izevbaye calls Achebe's first three novels including *Arrow of God* "studies in defeat" (143). Ezeulu's fall is a defeat in the ordinary sense. It represents the attempt of a strong character to apply his own inflexible will on society and his failure. But the novelist has added another major dimension to the character and his role. Achebe assigns to Ezeulu, "the magnificent man," the role of a victim of a historic situation. He points out that Ezeulu's fate is

> . . . perfectly consistent with his high historic destiny as victim, consecrating by his agony—thus raising to the status of a ritual passage—the defection of his people (Preface).

Ezeulu is elevated to the stature of victim—a martyr—against the background of the priest's commitment to their god, Ulu, and the people's desertion and defection in favour of a new god. His fall becomes a sacrifice with himself as the offering. His agony, according to the novelist, lends dignity and sanctity to the defection as it is an integral part of the sacrificial process during the period of social transition, or "passage" from one stage of existence to another.

Ezeulu's fall, along with that of his god, represents the irreversible victory of History over the uncompromising stand of Faith, resisting change in its realm. Historic destiny, in this case as well as in that of Elesin in *Death and the King's Horseman*, is accelerated by two major factors—the intervention of the white man and the personal defect of the protagonist which develops into the "tragic flaw."

The Chief Priest of Ulu, half man and half spirit, symbolizing spiritual authority over the people of his jurisdiction, is tortured by doubt--doubt over the range and nature of his power. This flaw, more than the white man's interference, is instrumental in his downfall:

> Whenever Ezeulu considered the immensity of his power over the year and the crops and, therefore, over the people he wondered if it was real. It was true he named the day for the Feast of the Pumpkin Leaves and for the New Yam feast; but he did not choose it. He was merely a watchman. . . . No! the Chief Priest of Ulu was more than that. If he should refuse to name the day there should be no festival—no planting and no reaping. But could he refuse? No Chief Priest had ever refused. So it could not be done. He would not dare (3).

The word "dare" holds the key to Ezeulu's tragic fall. He could not accept the obvious limitations to his power:

> Ezeulu was stung to anger by this as though his enemy had spoken it.
>
> 'Take away that word *dare*,' he replied to this enemy. 'Yes I say take it away. No man in all Umuaro can stand up and say that I dare not. The woman who will bear the man who will say it has not been born yet' (3).

The challenge to the "enemy" within himself questioning him whether he would "dare" becomes an obsession. Achebe conveys the very essence of Ezeulu's character with its inherent tragic irony in the beginning itself. The rest of the novel portrays how he works it out. He dares. He commits the act of *hubris*.

Ezeulu can be realistic in his thinking and is willing to adapt himself to situations of expediency. He agrees to send one of his sons, Oduche, to the Christian Missionary school, not because he is convinced of the value of the alien religion, but out of practical considerations:

> "The world is changing. . . . I do not like it. But I am like the bird Eneke-nti-oba. When his friends asked him why he was always on the wing he replied: 'Men of today have learnt to shoot without missing and so I have learnt to fly without perching.' I want one of my sons to join these people and be my eye there. If there is nothing in it you will come back. . . . My spirit tells me that those who do not befriend the white man today will be saying *had we known* tomorrow" (45-46).

As the spiritual representative of his clan he is more than an ordinary individual and becomes the agent and victim simultaneously. When he falls, he brings his people and his god down along with him. His friends had understood him well:

> ". . . A priest like Ezeulu leads a god to ruin himself. It has happened before."
>
> "Or perhaps a god like Ulu leads a priest to ruin himself" (213).

The god and the priest contribute to each other's ruin and fall together.

History has its own uncompromising part to play in this process of mutual destruction. Captain Winterbottom's message to Ezeulu with the idea of appointing him the Warrant Chief carried irony with it. It turned out to be even more ironic that the sudden attack of malaria prevents the District Officer from receiving Ezeulu, for whom he has genuine respect and concern. Instead, the pompous Mr. Clarke mishandles the situation and

Ezeulu finds himself under arrest. The outcome is that both the god and the priest fall from their pedestals. Ezeulu's brief reply to the white man reflects his defiance of the rulers as well as pride in his god whose authority alone he would represent:

> "Tell the white man that Ezeulu will not be anybody's chief, except Ulu" (175).

But his personal pride made him assert his authority and teach his clansmen a lesson for not having done anything to get him released. He was convinced that the balance of Nature and the rhythm of the seasons would be upset if he did not announce the suitable dates for important events like sowing and harvesting. He knew "his deity not seeing him in his place would ask Umuaro questions" (160).

Historic destiny begins to operate from another angle—that of religion. Exploiting the present crisis over the New Yam feast to his advantage, Mr. Goodcountry, Catechist of St. Marks C.M.S. Church, Umuaro, found it "an opportunity for fruitful intervention. . . . The New Year Festival was the attempt of the misguided heathen to show gratitude to God, the giver of all good things. This was God's hour to save them from their error which was now threatening to ruin them" (215). He encouraged the new converts to win over the people and added: "If Ulu who is a false God can eat one yam the living God who owns the whole world should be entitled to eat more than one" (216).

Ezeulu's clansmen comment on his role in the collapse: "The house he has been planning to pull down has caught fire and saved him the labour" (213). Ezeulu faces punishment in many forms. He loses his favourite son Obika in his attempt to appease Ulu; this aggravates his sense of loss and proves to be the final blow of fate which wrecks his sanity. Ezeulu, as Charles Larson observes, is "an extremely lonely man, a man of the strongest moral convictions who ultimately must stand alone in his decisions. . . . Achebe's concluding picture of the insane Ezeulu is indeed poignant, yet not unexpected" (152).

Obika's death upsets the equilibrium of Nature by reversing Order. The irony is hinted at in the traditional prayer to the new moon: "May children put their fathers into the earth, and not the fathers their children." Ezeulu raises the agonized cry:

> "Ulu, were you there when this happened to me?" (228).

His clansmen, at least the majority of them, felt that this would serve as a lesson for him: "This should teach him how far he could dare next time" (228).

Achebe portrays the fallen giant with sympathy and compassion:

> Think of a man who, unlike lesser men, always goes to battle without a shield because he knows that bullets and matchet strokes will glance off his medicine-boiled skin; think of his discovering in the thick of battle that the power has suddenly, without warning, deserted him. What next time can there be? (228).

His future is only that of a sacrificial ram whose agony caused by torture prior to sacrifice is as significant as the final beheading itself:

> Men had taken greater blows: that was what made a man a man. For did they not say that a man is like a funeral ram which must take whatever beating comes to it without opening its mouth; that the silent tremor of pain down its body alone must tell of its suffering? (229).

Pain compounded with humiliation makes him think in terms of proverbs. He wonders why Ulu had dealt with him in such a manner:

> When was it ever heard that a child was scalded by the piece of yam its own mother put in its palm? What man would send his son with a potsherd to bring fire from a neighbour's hut and then unleash rain on him? Who ever sent his son up the palm to gather nuts and then took an axe and felled the tree? (229).

As the agony deepens, Ezeulu realizes he is just an arrow to be shot by the god in any direction according to his will. The arrow itself has no choice. In this case, the arrow tried to adjust the direction to suit its own will, inviting tragedy.

The historical authenticity of Achebe's novels is conveyed effectively through the correct handling of the language with all its variations according to the context. Bernth Lindfors observes:

> What gives each of Achebe's novels an air of historical authenticity is his use of the English language (4).

A significant point of contrast between *Arrow of God* and *Death and the King's Horseman* is in the portrayal of the younger generation. Olunde, Elesin's son, is the key figure in the play, even towering over his father in moral stature. Achebe does not allow Ezeulu's sons to eclipse him, even though each of them is endowed with an individuality of his own. The low profile of the sons helps Ezeulu retain his stature. Soyinka, on the other hand, creates Olunde as a character overwhelming in his greatness, excelling even his father. Achebe maintains Ezeulu's superiority, and allows Obika's death to add poignancy to his suffering, but it does not elevate the son to the level of tragic grandeur. By offering himself to restore the lost balance, Soyinka's Olunde manages to maintain the equilibrium upset by his father's failure. Achebe elevates the tragic dignity of the protagonist; Soyinka adds to the poignancy of the situation.

Olunde represents the new generation with a renewed awareness of roots in the past, a better grasp of the present and a positive, clearer vision of the future than what has been displayed by the parents' generation. His is the most creative role as the saviour of the honour of his community and defender of ancestral faith at the cost of his own life. His conviction about the correctness of Yoruba wisdom has not been shaken. He knows England and Englishmen well, he intends to return and complete his medical studies. But in an ironic moment, dramatic to the highest degree, Olunde replaces his father as the loyal horseman who follows his king to the other world. Elesin shrinks, gets smaller and becomes a child in the presence of the young man, his son, who changes the order and precedes him in death. The son becomes the father. The father becomes younger than his son.

The historical factor, merely catalytic according to the dramatist, is conspicuous though placed in the background. Colonial administration carried with it repeated instances of political and personal intervention, conversion to Christianity, desecration of ancestral masks, indifference to the significance of indigenous customs and traditions and above all a sense of unquestioned superiority of the white man over the African.

Death and the King's Horseman is a paean to Death. Based on real events which took place in the ancient Nigerian city of Oyo in 1946, the play centres round the ritual suicide of the Chief, Elesin, the king's horseman, demanded by long-standing custom upon the death of the king. The serious repercussions triggered by the well-meaning intervention of Simon Pilkings, the British District Officer, testify to the intensity of Yoruba faith, the depth of which the alien mind could not assess.

The play is threnodic in essence yet festive in tone as it goes far beyond a conventional elegy. Soyinka sounds an appropriate warning against "the sadly familiar reductionist tendency" he has observed among critics, prompting them to misinterpret such works. He sounds a note of caution:

> The bane of themes of this genre is that they are no sooner employed creatively than they acquire the

> facile tag of 'clash of cultures', a prejudicial label which, quite apart from its frequent misapplication, presupposes a potential equality *in every given situation* of the alien culture and the indigenous, on the actual soil of the latter. . . . The Colonial Factor is an incident, a catalytic incident merely. The confrontation in the play is largely metaphysical, contained in the human vehicle which is Elesin and the universe of the Yoruba mind—the world of the living, the dead and the unborn, and the numinous passage which links all: transition (6-7).

Despite this emphasis on the metaphysical factor, the significance of the incident at a crucial moment in the history of Nigeria cannot be ignored. Whether it is the well-meaning intervention of the District Officer in this case, or the deliberate, calculated attempts at suppression, including large scale conversions to Christianity taking place elsewhere, the colonial factor raises its head, demanding attention. In all its poignancy, the metaphysical question is projected against the background of historical reality.

The depth of Elesin's faith in tradition can be gauged by the cheerful readiness with which he goes forward to embrace death in the fulfilment of his duty. He challenges the "Not-I" bird who weakens men's resistance to death, and makes cowards of everyone. The song of the "Not-I" bird represents Soyinka at the height of his lyrical inspiration. "Not-I" is the sudden response to Death's knock at the door. It is an aspect of human character: individuals who claim to be fearless echo the same protest, "Not-I". Elesin is shocked into disbelief; but he is different from the rest:

> I, when that Not-I bird perched
> Upon my roof, bade him seek his nest again,
> Safe, without care or fear. I unrolled
> My welcome mat for him to see. Not-I

Flew happily away (14).

Elesin is eager to keep up his tryst with Death. The "Not-I" bird would observe the mat unrolled to welcome Death. Elesin's approach to life is clear:

Life has an end. A life that will outlive
Fame and friendship begs another name (15).

A new dimension is added to the significance of the play by the sudden marriage arranged for Elesin at his own wish. Consummation of a new marriage when one is at the point of one's death would be incredible under normal circumstances, but to Elesin and to Iyaloja who represents traditional wisdom, it is very simple and logical. Nuptials and death appear sequential, conception itself being a link in the chain connecting two successive stages in the cycle of birth and death. The metaphysical dimension added to it can be explained in terms of the belief that the hero who goes into the other world in full glory should leave a part of himself behind in the form of a sprouting new life, to be born after the father's death. It is the privilege of the new bride not only to bear the child of honour, but to send the bridegroom off to the next world after the fulfilment of his earthly obligations. She alone should close his eyes with a pinch of fresh earth.

Such beliefs and customs, inherent in traditional Yoruba wisdom, could not be upheld without interference from the ruling white man. The latter's interference in *Arrow of God* is different in detail from the well-meaning ignorant intervention in *Death and the King's Horseman.*

Even Elesin is stunned at the cold touch of reality when Iyaloja announces with a finality characteristic of the Fates:

Now we must go prepare your bridal chamber,
Then these same hands will lay your shrouds (73).

Elesin fails at the crucial moment when Pilkings's men interrupt the ritual dance which would have taken him to the other world through self-induced hypnosis. He does not know whom to blame for his failure, and feels bewildered and demoralized. He expresses his view:

> First I blamed the white man, then I blamed my gods for deserting me. Now I feel I want to blame you for the mystery of the sapping of my will . . . my weakness came not merely from the abomination of the white man who came violently into my fading presence, there was also a weight of longing on my earth-held limbs (65).

Elesin recovers and explains the reason for the abomination brought on himself and his race:

> It is when the alien hand pollutes the source of will, when a stranger force of violence shatters the mind's calm resolution, this is when a man is made to commit the awful treachery of relief, commit in his thought the unspeakable blasphemy of seeing the hand of the gods in this alien rupture of his world (69).

Both Ezeulu and Elesin pass through this phase in the history of Nigeria when the alien hand "pollutes the source of will" resulting in the rupture of values. One of them blames the gods, but gods also fall in the process of collapse. The Praise-Singer emphasizes the same point:

> What the end will be, we are not gods to tell . . . our world is tumbling in the void of strangers, Elesin. . . (75).

Pilkings is exasperated and even a little unnerved by the

cool tenacity of the women who have gathered around Elesin who is under arrest. He fails to understand the riddles they speak in. He is eager to despatch Olunde back to England. He sends for Elesin's son. Iyaloja, the mother figure, adds to the complexity of the situation:

> Save your labour, white one. If it is the father of your prisoner you want, Olunde, he who until this night we knew as Elesin's son, he comes soon himself to take his leave (72).

Pilkings concedes defeat at the sight of Olunde's dead body and asks in a tired voice whether this was what they wanted. The mother replies, unruffled:

> No child, it is what you brought to be, you who play with strangers' lives, who even usurp the vestments of our dead, yet believe that the stain of death will not cling to you. The gods demanded only the old expired plantain but you cut down the sap-laden shoot to feed your pride (76).

The Englishman who fails to understand the situation is addressed as "child" by the Mother Figure, who had addressed Elesin similarly when he failed to live up to his undertaking, The "alien mind" could not fathom the depth of African wisdom and the firm faith which would never be shaken by modern education. The District Officer stands petrified, almost as a child, awe-struck. Faith triumphs through death, Change succeeds only in creating some temporary confusion.

The concept of life as an eternal continuum forming the cycle of births and deaths has been explained by Soyinka through the diagram of the tail-devouring snake, in the pattern of the "Mobius Strip". Yoruba wisdom is committed to the totality of the life-cycle, and not to earthly life which forms just a part of it. The same idea, on a much larger canvas, involving a number of generations belonging to different births had already been presented by Soyinka in his play *A Dance of the Forests*, connecting the past and the present with the half-born future in the form of the strange character, the Half Child.

Traditional Yoruba thought does not subscribe to a linear concept of time, but to a cyclic reality operating in the universe. Soyinka refers to certain parallel verities from Greek mythology:

> The expression 'the child is father of the man' becomes, within the context of this time-structure, not merely a metaphor of development, one that is rooted in a system of representative individuation, but a proverb of human continuity which is not uni-directional. Neither 'child' nor 'father' is a closed or chronological concept. The world of the unborn, in the Yoruba world-view, is as evidently older than the world of the living as the world of the living is older than the ancestor-world (*Myth* 10).

Soyinka realizes that modern man's vision is getting restricted in the course of his contact with novel thought processes. Olunde impresses us as the symbol of traditional wisdom resisting this influence.

The dramatist's caution that "the Colonial Factor is an incident, a catalytic incident merely" serves to forestall any temptation on the part of the critic to launch a detailed interpretation in terms of the contrast between Christianity and traditional Yoruba faith.

Music plays a very important role in *Death and the King's Horseman*, adding to the tempo of lyrical incantation throughout the play. Michael Etherton highlights the role of music in this contest:

> Within the play it is the means by which Elesin Oba, the King's Horseman, is supposed to commit his ritual suicide in honour of the dead Oba and so re-

> store harmony to the community which the death of the Oba has set at risk. Between the play and its audiences, music shows the far greater disharmony caused by his failure to commit suicide, and carries the audience through a far more profound crisis (260).

Music adds to the poignancy of the elegiac mood and elevates the play to a metaphysical level. The basic theme of life as an eternal continuum forms the quintessence of the final benediction:

> Now forget the dead; forget even the living.
> Turn your mind only to the unborn (76).

Death and the King's Horseman is a paean to Death in its ultimate glory celebrating death as an important link in the unbreakable chain of life.

History formulated on principles of challenge and response speaks through Achebe's novel with anthropological touches of realism. Soyinka's play introduces a crucial moment precipitated by the operation of the same principles, but adds metaphysical overtones as the crisis is a spiritual one for the nation.

Achebe's *A Man of the People* and Narayan's *The Guide:* A Contrastive Study

CHARLES PONNUTHURAI SARVAN

> But whereas Conrad may be forgiven . . . contemporary novelists (and film-makers) . . . have no excuse for their blindness. They have done their work *after* decolonization; *after* the massive intellectual, moral, and imaginative overhaul and deconstruction of Western representation of the non-Western world . . . *after* the novels and plays of Chinua Achebe, Ngugi wa Thiong'o, Wole Soyinka. . . . Western writers have maintained their biases in the *face* of history.
>
> (Edward Said, "Through Gringo Eyes: with Conrad in Latin America" 72).

If one can speak of Indo-Anglian literature, meaning works produced by Indians in English, then I suppose one can also speak of an Afro-Anglian literature—leaving aside the question debated off and on since the 1960s: "Who is an African?" (or, "Who is an *African* writer?"). Of the writers mentioned by Said, Ngugi cannot, and will not want to, be grouped with the Afro-Anglians. James Ngugi became Ngugi wa Thiong'o; he translated his works into Gikuyu, and now writes in his native language. (As I have said elsewhere, I use the term "native" without apology. It once caused offence but now it is more often a matter of pride, if not of contention, to be called a native.) Then there's Wole Soyinka: great playwright, novelist, poet essayist and Nobel Prize winner. Soyinka's brilliance and wit are difficult to match, and the attention he has attracted is amply deserved. But, based on almost fifteen years of teaching in African universities, I believe there is no Afro-Anglian writer who has had the impact of Achebe on the general reader and on students: he is read not only at the tertiary but also at the much wider secondary-school level; no writer who draws (unusual terms, no doubt, in the context of contemporary literary criticism) more regard and affection. I suspect Narayan enjoys something of the same reception among Indian readers. Achebe is likely to be remembered most for *Things Fall Apart* and *Arrow of God,* but here I wish to bring together his *A Man of the People* and Narayan's *The Guide.* There is a temptation when commenting on one author to make unfavourable comparisons with another; if writing on author X, to say how superior she or he is to Y in this or that way; when writing on Y, to say how much better or more interesting Y is than X. I will try to minimize invidious comparisons by stressing, and attempting to account for, differences.

"A man of the people" can mean "a man *for* the people," a championing which, in turn, suggests leadership: a role not far from that of a guide. However, both Chief Nanga and Raju are counterfeit: the latter becomes the *de facto* priest of an abandoned temple; the former is a fraudulent priest of politics, a precursor of characters such as we find in Ngugi's *The Trial of Dedan Kimathi* and *Devil on the Cross.* Both Achebe and Narayan are ironists—the latter more often so—and in *A Man of the People,* we have the irony of an irony in as much as Ibsen's character (in his *An Enemy of the People)* was anything but an enemy, whilst Nanga, the ostensible ally and friend of the people, is selfishly destructive of the community and the nation. In Raju, we have an ex-convict mistaken for, and treated with the respect and faith accorded to, a holy man: a man of sensuality taken for one who has abjured the world and all its deceitful and ephemeral blandishments. Whether these two frauds are similar, whether they have to deal with a gullible public, are questions that will be taken up later, but the very first page of each novel establishes the respective authors as master storytellers. (Achebe's is a first-person, retrospective narrative; Narayan uses the first-person narrator but also resorts to an extradiegetic, heterodiegetic voice.)

> Raju welcomed the intrusion—something to relieve the loneliness of the place. The man stood gazing reverentially on his face. Raju felt amused and embarrassed. "Sit down if you like", Raju said, to break the spell. The other accepted the suggestion with a grateful nod and went down the river steps to wash his feet and face, came up wiping himself dry with the end of a checkered yellow towel on his shoulder and took his seat two steps below the granite slab on which Raju was sitting cross-legged as if it were a throne, beside an ancient shrine. The branches of the trees canopying the river course rustled and trembled with the agitation of birds and monkeys settling down for the night. Upstream beyond the hills the sun was setting. Raju waited for the other to say something. But he was too polite to open a conversation.
>
> Raju asked, "Where are you from?" dreading lest the other should turn around and ask the same question (5).

A charming scene: an ancient shrine; distant hills (from which at the end the life-sustaining waters will flow down); the river (in which Raju will die); the birds and monkeys settling noisily and happily to sleep. But who are Raju and "the man"? (Note the use of the definite article, also known as the article of second-mention). Why does the man gaze "reverentially" at Raju and why should the latter dread being asked where he comes from? (Guilt? Shame?) Raju evidently thinks he does not deserve the excessive respect being accorded him—the man sits two steps below. Is it a case of mistaken identity? The reader is intrigued and involved. She or he is in the hands of a skilled novelist. So too with Achebe:

> No one can deny that Chief the Honourable M.A. Nanga, M.P., was the most approachable politician in the country. Whether you asked in the city or in his home village, Anata, they would tell you he was a man of the people. I have to admit this from the outset or else the story I'm going to tell will make no sense.
>
> That afternoon he was due to address the staff and students of the Anata Grammar School where I was teaching at the time. But as usual in those highly political times the villagers moved in and virtually took over. The Assembly Hall must have carried well over thrice its capacity. Many villagers sat on the floor, right up to the foot of the dais. I took one look and decided it was just as well we had to stay outside—at least for the moment.
>
> Five or six dancing groups were performing at different points in the compound. . . . In spite of the din you could still hear clear as a bird the high-powered voice of their soloist, whom they admiringly nicknamed 'Grammar-phone'. Personally I don't care too much for our women's dancing. . . (1).

Odili assumes the role of the oral narrator with the simple, "I am going to tell you a story," building expectancy and a link between himself and the reader (listener/participant). But simultaneously the author begins to distance us from, and to subvert, the narrator. The admission that Chief Nanga was "approachable" and popular is grudgingly made. (Envy?) The narrator is fastidious, feeling himself to be superior to the "common" people: "I took one look and decided it was just as well we had to stay outside". To him, the music is nothing but a "din";

there's snobbery, almost contempt, as he watches the women perform the traditional dances of welcome and joy; cheap laughter at those who mispronounce English words ("Grammar-phone" for gramophone). Odili wants us to align ourselves with him, to share his supercilious perspective and judgements; the author alerts and alienates, and so a complex interaction—beguiling surface simplicity—is set in motion.

Addressing ourselves to differences between *A Man of the People* and *The Guide*, Chief Nanga is crude, ruthless and insatiable in his craving for wealth and power. Success confirms and strengthens both his self-confidence and cynicism. In contrast—and unlike Soyinka's religious quacks—if Raju deceives the villagers, it is only to secure sufficient food for himself. (What he cannot consume, he returns to them: though, with a prudence painfully acquired, he keeps a small store against unforeseen eventualities.) As the hairdresser surmises, the crime for which he went to prison wasn't of a very serious nature: not on a national scale; not to an outrageous degree.

Achebe's first novel was *Things Fall Apart*, the story of a "centre" no longer able to hold society together; though a fraud, Raju turns the shrine into a place of peace and happiness, of *ananda* (delight of soul). He and the shrine become a "centre," one that the simple villagers needed, something not afar from the sphere of their sorrow and joys: soothing, answering and holding together. Finally, whether self-deceived, whether deluded by his own delusions or not, Raju attaches value to his words, redeems himself and, one is inclined to believe, saves the people. He dies a true man of the people. Turning to Odili, we find a man neither totally corrupt nor moral; he is sensitive and crude. He is unaware of his own contradictions and callowness; unaware that he was, whilst with Nanga, seduced by power and wealth and, with Max, had started on the slippery path of political expediency and compromise. In contrast, Raju acquires a fair degree of self-knowledge and can be harsh in his judgement of himself.

More importantly, Achebe's work is different in that whilst Narayan's is the perceptive, humorous portrayal of an individual, *A Man of the People* deals with a people, their life and politics (with a bitterness absent from *The Guide)*, and the story is marked by violent upheaval, by social and political chaos. In Narayan's novel, there is comedy even towards the end: it is the misunderstanding of a frightened simpleton which commits Raju to his fast, and it takes the nonplussed Guide a while to find out what he himself is supposed to have said. His urgent confession to Velan, far from saving him, enhances respect—past profligacy serving to heighten present piety—and leaves him without escape. One may object, saying that Achebe's work also has its touches of comedy: for example, the scene where the Honourable Simon Koko believes he's been poisoned, is hilarious caricature. (The Minister's imported coffee having run out, the cook had used a locally processed variety, had bought "OHMS"—Our Home Made Stuff):

> Chief Koko . . . proceeded to take a loud and long sip. . . . Then he practically dropped the cup and saucer . . . and jumped up as though a scorpion had stung him. . . .
>
> "What is the use of a doctor?" moaned our poisoned host. "Do they know about African poison? They have killed me. What have I done to them? Did I owe them anything? Oh! Oh! Oh! What have I done?" (37-38).

But humour gives way to sombreness when we are told of the campaign mounted by the same government ministers, urging people to consume local products in the national interest. At the end, armed gangs terrorize the populace and the opportunist army stages a coup, taking over what's left of "the national cake" for itself, though in the guise of saving the country.

Achebe's is a pained satire, and there is no comparison in nature and degree between the deceit of Raju and that of Nanga. That *A Man of the People* is about corruption—insatiable, devoid of conscience, lacking any sympathy for the poor who form the vast majority of the population—is evident, has been commented upon often, and need not be dwelt upon here. (For parallels in real life, we can think of Mobutu in Africa or Marcos in Asia.) *A Man of the People* is known as one of the early "post-colonial disillusionment novels." Nanga is a fraud not only in political and commercial terms but also culturally. He attacks those Africans who have received a Western education, poses and parades as a champion of an "authentic" African culture but he hankers after, and fills his house with, things Western. He prefers to speak English, and his children are well on the way to losing their mother-tongue. Despite the overt aggression and bluster, the years of colonialism have bred feelings of inferiority, and the inability to be ever fully like the erstwhile masters. A young American couple is permitted—tacitly encouraged—to be familiar with Nanga, and he is not only pleased but *flattered*:

> A car drew up outside and a young American couple breezed in. . . .
>
> "Hi Micah, hi Margaret," said the woman. . . . But he seemed quite pleased. . . . These two people were no older than I and yet had the impudence to call Chief Nanga his now almost forgotten Christian name. . . . I had turned quickly and anxiously to watch his face contort with fury. But no. He had replied sweetly . . . if I or any of our people for that matter had called him Micah he would have gone rampaging mad. . . . We have all accepted things from white skins that none of us would have brooked from our own people (49).

Max's poem laments historical exploitation and depredation:

> I will return home to her—many centuries have I wandered—
> And I will make my offering at the feet of my lovely

> Mother:
> I will rebuild her house, the holy places they raped
> and plundered,
> And I will make it fine with black wood, bronzes and
> terra-cotta (91).

The "they" of the song (3rd line) implies foreigners, but the destruction (economic and cultural) is continued by the heroes of independence.

Politicians are few, the people many, and in them is hope supposed to repose. In *The Guide*, the folk are innocent, trusting, essentially kind and decent. It is their simplicity, their faith in religion and trust in him which compel Raju to attach value to his words: it is they who change him. From this we turn to the people in Achebe's novel. The first paragraph of the novel concludes: "they would tell you he was a man of the people. I have to admit this . . . or else the story I'm going to tell will make no sense" (1). So too, we must know the people in order to make sense of their man—and vice versa. Initially, they seem foolish and gullible, repeatedly deceived by the vulgar, blatantly false politicians. They do not think they have claims on the nation's wealth or on state property, and if funds are misappropriated and holdings damaged or misused, they see no link between such doings and the lack of amenities in towns and villages, the poor or non-existent transport system, the lack of proper schools, medical centres and job-opportunities. Later, we see them as tired and apathetic:

> Max began by accusing the outgoing Government of all kinds of swindling and corruption. As he gave instance after instance . . . many in the audience laughed. But it was the laughter of resignation to misfortune. No one among them swore vengeance; no one shook with rage or showed any sign of fight. They understood what was being said, they had seen it with their own eyes. But what did anyone expect

> them to do? (139).

Later still, we see them as cynical: "Some political commentators have said it was the supreme cynicism of these transactions that inflamed the people and brought down the Government. That is sheer poppycock. The people themselves . . . had become even more cynical than their leaders and were apathetic into the bargain" (161). In a situation where there is no morality either in public conduct or in private life, they scramble to gather up crumbs from under the table, waiting for opportunities, wishing, each one, to be as successful as Nanga—and never mind the price in morality or the damage to the public. Odili, himself no model of conduct, is at pains to clarify that the people had nothing to do with the coup which swept away the government:

> No, the people had nothing to do with the fall of our Government. What happened was simply that unruly mobs and private armies having tasted blood and power during the election had got out of hand and ruined their masters and employers. And they had no public reason whatever for doing it. Let's make no mistake about that (162).

It is this disappointment with the people—more serious in the long run than the criminality of the Nangas—which explains the novel's bitterness, and the concluding lines:

> Max was avenged not by the people's collective will but by one solitary woman who loved him. Had his spirit waited for the people to demand redress it would have been waiting still, in the rain and out in the sun. . . . I say, you died a good death if your life had inspired someone to come forward and shoot your murderer in the chest—*without asking to be paid* (167. My emphasis).

The title, *A Man of the People*, is invariably seen as being ironic, Nanga being an enemy of the community and the nation, but I would argue that the irony is that there is no irony, for Nanga is a truly representative specimen: he comes from the people and is like them. In this sense, he *is* a man of the people. In a democracy, we are told, a people get the government they deserve, and, as events in Eastern Europe have shown almost three decades after the publication of this work, change can be encompassed even under harshly efficient dictatorships, if the necessary political awareness and will are found. The title consists of two noun phrases joined by a preposition (and meaning both "for" and "from") but, of them, the great tragedy emerges from the portrayal of the second. It is the people, Achebe argues, who must force politicians and politics to change.

Within a society and at a given time, two writers can differ very much in subject, perception and mood. Therefore, the differences between African Achebe and Asian Narayan need not surprise us. Perhaps Achebe's anger (see also his essay, *The Trouble with Nigeria)* is bitter because writers (and critics) are often most uncompromising when dealing with their societies—because they care and want better, if not the best, for their own. Conrad described revolutionary success as leading to the betrayal of hopes and the caricaturing of ideals. If so, the African answer to betrayal can be summed up in "A Luta Continua"—and her writers are in the forefront of the continuing struggle.

But having said this, one must admit that poverty, gross economic inequality, political hypocrisy, corruption are no less evident in India than in Africa. Then why isn't there in Indo-Anglian literature (perhaps with the exception of Anand) the sadness and anger of an Armah (especially in his The *Beautyful Ones Are Not Yet Born)*, the fierce indignation of a Ngugi—or an Achebe? Why the African writer is so much more angry, and committed to encompassing positive change, I do not claim to be able to explain. Is it that African societies, being younger, are also more vigorous, impatient and demanding? Does the Hindu belief in re-birth--that the sufferings of this life are the direct and just consequence of misconduct in a past existence—breed not only poise, equanimity and stoicism, but also resignation, passivity and acquiescence? Stagnation can easily be confused with stability.

As historians have recorded, Westerners sought to justify their imperialism and racism by minimizing the culture and worth of the conquered peoples. A common and equal humanity was forgotten or denied: people were treated differently simply because they were different in colour, culture or level of technological development. However, in India there was ample evidence of once strong and great civilizations. The tactic, therefore, was to speak of Indian degeneracy (from this ancient glory). In Africa, Europeans believed they confronted not decline but absence or worse, a Manichean darkness. Africans were the most insulted of peoples and, as Achebe says, their very humanity was called into question. Africans were thought to be without culture, and many Africans accepted this evaluation: p'Bitek's Ocol asks in anguished humiliation: mother, why was I born black? It is when the subjected accept deep within themselves, consciously or not, the inferiority foisted on them, that the damage is complete. We think of Okara's image of cultural "uprooters" with their spades; of Okigbo's gods lying derelict behind the shrine room; of Diop's Westernized African who affects a European accent, and even tries to blush. The list can be lengthened—see Max's song already quoted—but the point, I trust, is taken. In India, there perhaps isn't that sense of things having completely fallen apart, of a massive foreign undermining. Max's song laments the years of cultural exile: Raju never left. And Rosie, despite her name, "fostered our cultural traditions" (9). A classical dancer, she practises hard and devotedly. Hinduism and Indian culture remain largely undamaged, changing under their own dynamism rather than through foreign interference. For example, Christianity is practised but by a comparatively small minority.

It is from this insult and damage that African societies

fought for and won their independence. Then to see that freedom (a beginning and an opportunity) hijacked and perverted by native leaders is infuriating and not to be countenanced. Traditional society was attacked and vilified, and the present is marked by moral pusillanimity and, worse, by unbridled greed and rampant corruption. (The term "underdeveloped" has now been replaced by the more hopeful-sounding "developing," but many countries are regressing rather than developing.) This background may help to explain the African writer's anger and commitment to change: conquest and extremely contemptuous treatment for centuries; loss of individual and collective confidence; effort and sacrifice leading to independence; hopes for the future; the cruel thwarting of potential; the disappointment of expectations and dreams. The present morass is not unique to black African countries but the context sketched out above may help to explain the exceptionally strong (literary) reaction.

Comparisons, I said at the beginning, are invidious, but they are not always avoidable, nor should we be afraid to make them. Achebe's subject matter is of the utmost importance: the historical encounter with the West, the destruction of the traditional way of life, the portrayal and analysis of the unhappy present. Achebe, grappling with fundamentals at the national level, is important to his fellow Africans in a way which I wonder if Narayan is to his readership. To suggest an analogy, while Jane Austen is not only delightful but also subtle and perceptive, Lawrence is more urgent and reaches down to deeper, and more wide-ranging analyses. Even if his understanding and "answers" are not entirely satisfactory, the problems he confronted and drew attention to, are vital. Whether this analogy is appropriate or not, I leave to Indian critics to judge.

Returning to Achebe, *Things Fall Apart* is the first title in the Heinemann African Writers Series, a place it deserves not merely on grounds of publishing history and chronological accident. Translated into over forty languages, Achebe's novels both create and alter awareness. In words now famous, he set out to espouse a revolution—no less than to help his society regain belief in itself, and thus put away the complexes bred by years of denigration and self-abasement. What more difficult challenge, what higher ideal can a writer set himself? Literature here is raised to high seriousness, without loss of aesthetic "delight." Achebe can claim to have had a positive influence on the thinking of his fellow Nigerians, on their awareness of the past, and on their understanding of the present. By extension, he has had an influence on Africans, on non-Western and Western readers. To return to the epigraph, it is right that Edward Said, listing those very few who have made a significant contribution to knowledge in and of the non-Western world, should mention Chinua Achebe: a man from the people, speaking to the peoples of *both* worlds.

Parallels and Pointers: Patterns in the African and Indian Postcolonial Experience

CYNTHIA VANDEN DRIESEN

"Our discipline is now spending so much time critiquing colonialist discourse that the genuinely new directions implicit in the study of the new literatures in English are being neglected. . . . Deconstructing imperialism keeps us within imperialism's orbit. . ." (Brydon 23). Diana Brydon's suggestion that we need to attend to the variety of writers' voices speaking from different positions within the field and to start with these rather than Derrida, Lacan or Todorov as a means of "reconfiguring our sense of the possibilities and dilemmas of our enterprise" appears to be a timely one. It could be that theoretical debates have dissipated energies so that interesting lines of comparison between the works of literary artists drawn from widely different cultures yet linked by the cataclysmic experience of colonialism and their common use of the English language (or an "english") have not been explored (Ashcroft, Griffiths, Tiffin 38-77). Comparative studies in the field are sparse considering the period over which it has now engaged critical attention (Jeffares 24).

As Said has indicated (and Brydon herself notes) one's own position in relation to the field is of some significance (*Orientalism* 25). Compiling my own "inventory of traces" would involve a recognition of the mixture of influences in my background which would tend to produce a kind of hybrid. Now an Australian citizen, I am of Sri Lankan origin and the product of a Western-oriented educational system and life experiences which have involved teaching and studying for extended periods in Asia, Africa and Australia. Years ago the Indian novelist and critic Balachandra Rajan suggested that "the man with mixed allegiances is contemporary Everyman" (108). The post-colonial literatures particularly offer the possibilities of exploring this idea; of highlighting striking similarities and significant differences between the experiences of the hybrid products which are the inevitable result of the clash of cultures subsumed under the term colonialism. These are emphases which should not be disregarded if we are to rediscover through the discourse on those literatures, those "humanistic values" which Said has shown that Orientalism "by its scope, experiences and structures, has all but eliminated" (*Orientalism* 110).

Some of these writers, perhaps because of the consistency of their preoccupations and the substance of their achievement, have acquired a recognizable role almost as chroniclers of their people's experience. Chinua Achebe indeed saw his work as affording Nigerians the opportunity "to look back and try and find out where we went wrong, where the rain began to beat us" (*Morning* 44). India's R.K. Narayan in a career spanning over five decades has produced a group of novels that provide striking insights into a crucial phase of Indian experience. Comparison of a work by each of these writers clearly set in the postcolonial era promotes an awareness of striking similarities as well as some aspects of remarkable difference. They reflect in some measure, through the dilemmas of the central characters, attempts of these societies to readjust as it were, after the shock of the colonial experience, a shock which for these traditional societies was also synonymous with the beginnings of their advent into the modern technological age.

Despite their widely different cultural contexts there is an essential kinship of experience and outlook between Achebe's Odili in *A Man of the People* and Narayan's Raju in *The Guide*. Odili is obviously a later mutation of Obi Okonkwo of *No Longer At Ease*, more amoral, more detached from the claims of family, tribe or religion. Raju, more strikingly than other Narayan protagonists, appears similarly liberated from restrictions of traditional beliefs and observances. For both, self-interest appears the only guide to conduct. Odili's involvement in politics grows simply out of his desire to be revenged on Chief Nanga for the humiliation over his girlfriend, as earlier his moral objections to the politician dissolve easily at his invitation to the city and the prospect of an easy scholarship. Raju has no compunction in posing as a holy man since it ensures an easy livelihood at the expense of the poor villagers, as earlier he commits forgery to ensure continuance of his luxurious lifestyle through the exploitation of the woman he supposedly loves. In fact both these antiheroes acquire the distinct aspects of parasites. Odili seems less adept than Chief Nanga at exploiting others at the start, but by the end of this deeply pessimistic novel he has learnt from the master, and party funds will be diverted to pay his bride-price for Edna without a qualm on his part.

For both young men the ties of family, of religion, of tradition are meaningless. If the mother-figure in traditionally oriented societies is presented as the repository of tradition, it is interesting to note the presentation of this figure in these novels. Obi Okonkwo's mother (in Achebe's earlier novel) is an ailing woman but her significance as spokesperson for the traditional order is underlined when she remonstrates with her son on his decision to marry an outcaste woman. Later Obi experiences a sense of relief at her death. Significantly in this later novel, Odili's mother has died in childbirth and he is taunted as the "bad child that crunched his mother's skull" (32). His father is also identified with the alien power, having been a District Interpreter.

Raju's position in relation to this mother-figure appears only marginally different. She is compelled to leave the house when he insists that Rosie lives with them and the rout of tradition appears complete. Yet unlike in Achebe's work, this rout is later shown to be only temporary. One recalls then that Raju's mother has remained as a central figure in the household for several years and the grown man Raju is deeply moved: "I had seen her for years at the same time sitting with closed eyes . . . it now filled me with sadness that I should not see her there any more'' (155).

To continue, for the moment, to trace the broad parallels between these young men, each reveals even in his pursuit of his romantic interests, the same amoral self-interest, even a kind of calculated callousness that undercuts any suggestion of idealism or romance. Neither is deterred by the fact that the woman he is attracted to is legally or morally committed to another man—her husband in Rosie's case, her fiancé in Edna's. Traditional taboos are equally meaningless. So Raju is unaffected by the fact that Rosie comes from the caste of temple dancers, while Odili is unconcerned that Chief Nanga has already paid the bride-price for Edna. Both adopt a calculated, deliberate kind of strategy, trying out particular tactics and detachedly assessing their success. Having decided that he would ''go back, seek out Nanga's parlour-wife, and give her the works, good and proper'' (86), Odili observes the effect of his early moves: ''She was not in the least surprised by my offer. She was obviously the trusting type—which augured well'' (105). Raju assesses his progress in the seduction of Rosie with similar calculation: ''I praised her dancing. I spoke out my love but sandwiched it conveniently between my appreciations of her art. . . . It worked'' (74). Each seems to experience some degree of genuine attraction to his mistress but this seems subordinated at will to his own self-love. Raju suppresses information about her husband from Rosie and commits forgery rather than risk his luxurious lifestyle; Odili unleashes a stream of calculated insults in a letter as the only possible revenge when he thinks he is losing Edna.

Within each novel the writer presents a sketch of the more traditional woman beside which the portrait of the ''new'' woman who engrosses the young man's attention must also be measured. In both, remarkably, the traditional figure appears appreciative of the ''New'' woman's achievements. Mrs Nanga accepts philosophically (except for one outburst) the idea of her being too unfashionable and insufficiently educated and refers to

Edna as "our" wife. The criteria for the selection of the "parlour-wife" are education and good looks. Yet even Odili registers a sense of the vitality and strength of Mrs Nanga. Her abuse of him after his betrayal of Chief Nanga leaves him more shaken than the encounter with Nanga himself. Edna actually appears naive in comparison to Mrs Nanga and seems far more dominated by the male figures in her experience.

In fact women, despite their careers as lawyers or nurses in the new society, still seem tied to subordinate roles as sex objects to the men they encounter. Even the "most sophisticated-looking young woman" introduced to Odili as "Barrister Mrs Akilo" provokes the following reaction:

> I must confess to a certain awkwardness before her sophisticated, assured manner. The way she spoke she must have spent her childhood in England. But this awkward feeling was only momentary. After all, I told myself, Chief Nanga who was barely literate was probably going to sleep with her that night (53).

Yet it is one of these new, young, educated women who is also recorded as making the only significant gesture of protest against the general deterioration of the nation's moral and political life. Reflecting on Max's fiancee's avenging of his death, even Odili concludes that

> Max was avenged not by the people's collective will but by one solitary woman who loved him. . . . For I do honestly believe that in the fat-dripping, gummy, eat-and-let-eat regime just ended . . . you died a good death if your life had inspired someone to come forward and shoot your murderer in the chest—without asking to be paid (167).

The world reflected particularly with regard to the status of women is very much a world in transition in both novels. In the venal city, Odili competes with Nanga for the favours of amenable females. While at one stage apparently discounting the traditional observance with regard to the formal procedures of marriage when he wishes to persuade Edna she has no obligation to marry Nanga, he later exploits these practices when it seems they would serve his purpose. He formally establishes his own claims to Edna through paying the traditional bride-price—but shows again the cynical amoral consciousness of the new generation in his cool decision to use party funds. "I had already decided privately to borrow the money from CPC funds still in my hands. They were not likely to be needed soon" (165).

A similar medley of figures fills the background of Raju's life in Narayan's novel. The traditional figure of the mother waiting obediently on her husband's pleasure and abiding by the advice of older male relatives or faithfully serving the household gods, is drawn with considerable sympathy. Like Mrs Nanga, the traditional female figure in Achebe's novel, Raju's mother, one notes, is not without an appreciation of the value of education and its potential. She is thoroughly approving of Rosie's having gained a Master's degree in Economics, declaring "You are not like us uneducated women. You will get on anywhere" (126).

The peculiar mixture of tradition and modernity that characterizes both novels, especially in their portrayal of the roles of women and marriage and match-making in their different societies, is particularly apparent in the case of Rosie. As an intellectual Marco had shown himself sufficiently uncaring of traditional taboos to marry a woman belonging to the caste of temple dancer, and Rosie's possession of a Master's degree offsets the traditional disqualification. After marriage he appears to treat her as something less than human as she comes a poor second to his complete absorption in his work. Raju cunningly establishes his hold upon her through exploiting her genuine passion for her own art and through promising to further her career as a dancer. Later after his unprincipled exploits lead him into the Law-Courts he recognizes that Rosie possesses enough resilience to continue without his help. More convincingly perhaps than in Achebe's novel, Narayan's projects a sense of the potential of the new woman. Economic independence appears to be the key factor as Raju realizes: "I was now a sort of hanger-on in the house; ever since she had released me from police-custody, the mastery passed to her" (195).

The existence of an older way of life alongside the growing manifestations of the new adds piquancy to the settings of these novels. One encounters that curious amalgam of lingering tradition and invading modernity that can perhaps only be appreciated fully by those who have had some direct experience of living in these cultures. It is finally this context of living that provides the backdrop for the development of the new hybrid anti-hero and must therefore in some way provide a part explanation of why and how he is what he is.

In Achebe's novel the opening sentence immediately focuses on the significant conjunction: "No one can deny that Chief the Honourable M.A. Nanga M.P., was the most approachable politician in the country" (1). The juxtaposition of the tribal title alongside the Western honorific of the imported British political system sets the keynote for the way of life subsequently portrayed in the novel. The previous section has already highlighted the blur of confused situations relating to women and to marriage. It is no exaggeration to note that this mixture of elements is present in all the facets of life presented—food, clothing, housing and the whole range of social and personal relationships and interactions.

Odili's father regales himself with "a jar of palm-wine every morning and a bottle of schnapps now and again" (35). In his "peace offering" to his father, Odili is obliged to include "a bottle of schnapps, two bottles of White Horse and a bottle of Martell" (35). Apparently unconscious of any irony Chief Nanga rejects Chief Koko's offer of tea or coffee as drinks for "black white-men" and suggests "whisky and soda for me and Mr Samalu" (37). Since this is the era after independence, Chief Nanga is splendidly garbed in traditional robes. He takes the young writer Jalio to task for his unconventional dress. "Either you wear a suit . . . or if you don't like it you can wear our national costume" (70).

Ensconced in the comfort of his suite in the Minister's home Odili reflects:

> The surprises and contrasts in our great country were simply inexhaustible. Here was I in our capital city, reading about pails of excrement from the cosy comfort of a princely seven bathroom mansion with its seven gleaming, silent action, water closets (46).

Social events reveal the same mixture of influences. Christmas is celebrated with a presentation by masked dancers. The degeneration of the tribal past is perhaps most poignantly presented here when the rope ostensibly restraining the Mask comes undone!

> One might have expected this sudden access to freedom to be followed by a wild rampage and loss of life and property. But the Mask tamely put his matchet down, helped his disciples retie the rope, picked up his weapon again and resumed his dance (109).

The ultimate status symbol in the new society is, of course, the motor car. Odili's father despises his son's meanly paid occupation: "He would . . . tell me [Odili] for the hundredth time to leave 'this foolish teaching' and look for a decent job in the government and buy myself a car" (35). Certainly Odili experiences the fact that "In our country a long American car driven by a white-uniformed chauffeur and flying a ministerial flag could pass through the eye of a needle" (65). The Americans have indeed arrived on the Nigerian scene. Achebe's portrayal of the American presence—their desire to befriend, to please the "locals" and (perhaps, unwittingly) to patronize them, is etched with a light but pointed satire.

Narayan's novels, written over a period of fifty years, reflect subtly the variety of changing features in the Indian scene. In *The Guide* the changes over years are quite effectively telescoped into the one novel. From the idyllic country scenes of Raju's boyhood, Malgudi develops rapidly into a busy town where tourists arrive daily by train on the newly built railway. Shops, theatres, photographic studios develop apace. Modernity and tradition coexist visibly and the relics of the Raj are now sights for the tourist along with archaeological artefacts of interest to scholars. In the closing scenes of the novel the American arrives with his television camera placating, seemingly considerate, but ultimately exploitative. Raju, now the holy man, reacts with traditional dignity where the younger Raju's reaction one feels would more nearly have resembled Odili's mixed feelings of attraction and hostility as he felt himself obscurely challenged by this latest mutation of the colonial power and the forces of modernization.

Raju's father had acquired a horse and carriage which had made him "the talk of the town" (34) but throughout the main events Gaffur's taxi features most significantly and the trains whose coming had only been foreshadowed at the beginning thunder through Malgudi bringing more visitors, more business, more complications in their wake. His father's house had been built by his own hands:

> He had dug the earth, kneaded the mud with water and roofed them with coconut thatch. He planted papaya trees around . . . a single fruit brought him eight annas if carved with dexterity (10).

Raju at the height of his career enjoys a lifestyle suited to a modern entrepreneur of the first rank:

> The stylish house at New Extension was more in keeping with our status. It was two-storied, with a

> large compound, lawns, garden, and garage. . . . I had a large staff of servants—a driver . . . two gardeners . . . a Gurkha sentry . . . and two cooks. . . (166).

Raju revels in being able to serve his guests whiskey in a land of prohibition. Like his Nigerian counterparts he recognizes this as a mark of status. Throughout his varied career Raju's dress consistently presents that eccentric combination of East and West that seems so characteristic of his world. As tourist guide he wears a Khaki bush-coat and *dhoti*. Late in his role as impresario, besides silk shirt and *dhoti* he sports "rimless glasses—(a present from Marco)" and a wristwatch (157).

In postcolonial India there is also the sense of a resurgence in indigenous Indian art. Rosie begins her meteoric rise to fame with Raju's successful persuasion of the local school Committee to set aside "the usual Shakespeare tragedy" in favour of an Indian dance recital at their annual social. One of those minor points of contrast between Raju and Odili is the former's positive feeling for his country's art. He appears genuinely moved by the aesthetic appeal of Nalini's performance:

> It [the snake-dance] was her masterpiece. Every inch of her body from toe to head rippled and vibrated to the rhythm of the song which lifted [her] into a creature of grace and divinity and an ornament of the gods. . . . I was captivated by it (184).

Achebe's satirical sketch of the Minister of Culture presiding at the function of the Writer's Society, humiliating the young writer Jalio by comments on his unorthodox dress and carelessly displaying his ignorance of the country's best-known writer requires little comment. Odili's behaviour is not more edifying. He feels himself humiliated when young Jalio shows he has no recollection of their earlier acquaintance and is simply distracted for the rest of the time:

> I didn't listen much to Chief Nanga's speech. When Elsie and I were not whispering into each other's ears I was thinking about the night or even about such irrelevant things as the dress of some of the people in the room. . . (71-72).

Because of their use of a first-person narrator the language of the novels is itself an important contributory element in establishing an insight into the central character. In Achebe's novel, in which the first-person narrator is used consistently, this is particularly marked. Narayan's pure and limpid style has been frequently commented on by the critics. This derives partly from the relative sparsity of untranslated words (though a few of these—e.g. *dhoti*, *pyol*—occur) and the lack of a significant attempt to superimpose local dialectal rhythms or syntactical structures upon standard English in the manner of most postcolonial writers endeavouring to evoke the sense of a specific cultural location.

With the recurrent flashbacks, the novel is so structured that we hear the recognizable tones of Raju recounting his past adventures and his cynical humour pervades these sections. The language acquires a marked colloquial flavour as when he expresses his annoyance at Marco:

> What does he take me for, this fellow, telling me that he wanted the car at this hour or at that hour—did he think I was a tout? It made me very angry, but the fact was that I really was a tout, having no better business than hanging around. . . (61).

The shallow cynical tone of Raju militates against any suggestion of a depth of feeling. Note his account of the growing estrangement between himself and Rosie:

> We were going through a set of mechanical actions day in and day out . . . fussy organizers . . . the same

> middle sofa in the first row . . . congratulations and off to catch the train—pocketing the most important thing—the cheque (172).

The relative neutrality of the style enables the author to procure an unobtrusive (and diplomatic) distancing of Raju's consciousness as the forces of spiritual regeneration begin to work in him. The final presentation of Raju the saint immolating himself for his people is therefore presented effectively from the viewpoint of the all-knowing narrator.

The language in Achebe's novel works consistently as a mode of revelation of characters. Achebe's use of Odili as narrator means the tones of this morally and emotionally dehydrated anti-hero recur throughout. Arthur Ravenscroft describes him as "self-accused" in the rotten society of *A Man of the People*, primarily through his own language: "the words themselves reveal a shallow personality" (122-23). Note the flat pedestrian description of the events of the evening leading to his break-up with Nanga:

> I retired soon after dinner so that the others might take the cue. And Elsie did. The second time I peeped out she was no longer there in the sitting-room. But Chief Nanga sat on stolidly looking at the file of the speech he had already given. Every two minutes or so I came to the door and peeped out. . . (77).

His reaction to his betrayal can only be conveyed in cliches, "I was transfixed to the spot. . . . What went on in my mind at that time lacked form and I cannot now set it down. . ." (77). The ending is simply bathetic:

> I did not think anything particularly. I just bit my lower lip until it was sore. Occasionally words like 'Good Heavens' escaped me and came out aloud. . .

'My word!' I remember saying. . . (79) .

The language itself establishes the personality as shallow, emotionally impoverished.

Usually, the occurrence of pidgin in the postcolonial text indicates a form of communication between classes, of ruler and ruled (in the earlier context of British rule) or later between the privileged, educated and the uneducated and unprivileged. Nanga and Chief Koko speak to their cooks in this manner. Yet often the use of pidgin between social equals here seems to suggest a special collusion in wrongdoing, a kind of deliberate refusal to recognize codes of correct behaviours. So Chief Nanga addresses his brother politician Chief Koko in pidgin as he swaps stories of his amorous conquests with Odili in the same medium.

In Achebe's earlier novels the introduction of Igbo proverbs into the language works towards incorporating a sense of native rhythms and syntactic structures, creating thereby a sense of the cultural distinctiveness of the context. In those novels which recreate the Igbo past it is an important means of establishing a sense of the wisdom and richness of that past. In the "modern" novels there is a hollowness of effect. Gareth Griffiths has shown how they underline a sense of the growing inadequacy of the proverbial language to function in a world whose desires are framed in directly opposed terms (98). So the proverb relating to the punishment of the man who took so much that the owner noticed had a relevance in the traditional context where some amount of wealth is recognizably communal but as Odili realizes "in the affairs of the nation there was no owner, the laws of the village became powerless" (167).

If the city is synonymous with the technological modern civilization of the West, the village remains in every culture the last stronghold of the traditional communal life. In its simplest terms Raju's spiritual regeneration is secured by his actual physical removal from the corrupting influences of the town to the relatively unspoiled life of the village. The simple faith and piety of the villagers are the prime factors in transforming the ex-convict into the saint (vanden Driesen 166-70). Raju rediscovers in the village the integrated existence which fell apart in the life of the towns as a result of the contact with the West. Daily the villagers repair to the feet of the "holy man" and absorb his words in the shrine by the river. Raju himself recognizes that the strength of this humble piety in Velan is itself the ultimate threat to him:

> Every respectful word that this man employed pierced Raju like a shaft. "He will not leave me alone," Raju thought with resignation, "This man will finish me. . ." (209).

Achebe's novel portrays no such survival of a reservoir of traditional pieties. The new values of materialism and individual self-interest have invaded the village as well. The village of Anata is solidly behind the corrupt Nanga and (a direct reversal of the pattern of events in Narayan's novel), Odili's first acquaintance with the wily politician takes place in the village. When he abandons his job as village teacher to sample the opportunities of the big city, his moral destruction is ensured. Apparently the Minister sends his children to the village periodically. As Mrs Nanga explains, "Without it . . . they would become English people" (43). Other details show however that the city values have invaded the village. Take the instance of the returning students:

> We call them holiday makers and their presence has a way of immediately raising the general tone of the village, giving it an air of well-dressed sophistication. The boys I saw that morning wore Italian-type shoes and tight trousers and the girls wore lipstick and hair stretched with hot iron. . . (107).

It is in this survival of the village and particularly of the religious traditions within it that the postcolonial scene as portrayed in Narayan's novel contrasts with Achebe's portrayal of the Nigerian scene. In *No Longer at Ease* Achebe had already shown how lightly Christian religious beliefs sat upon the convert Nwoye's son Obi Okonkwo, *Arrow of God* had presented the traditional priest's recognition of what the coming of Christianity had portended. In the post-British era the Christian ethic appears as of little relevance as the traditional. Max's idealism (for which he is shot) has absolutely no relation to the fact of his being the son of a Christian missionary; he does not subscribe to his father's beliefs. Religion whether Christian or traditional is not a factor of any consideration to Odili. The only religious image of any significance emerges in the satirical lines of the last paragraph of the novel describing the corruptness of the era just past:

> a regime in which you saw a fellow cursed in the morning for stealing a blind man's stick and later in the evening saw him again mounting the altar of the new shrine in the presence of all the people to whisper into the ear of the chief celebrant. . . (167).

It is not that the new influences have not been felt on the Indian scene. The young Raju is impatient with the religious rituals so important to his parents but puts on a performance calculated to impress his watchful father:

> I washed myself at the well, smeared holy ash on my forehead, stood before the framed picture of gods . . . and recited all kinds of sacred verse in a loud, ringing tone. . . (11).

Later as a young man about town he becomes involved with a young married woman who belongs to the taboo caste of temple dancers. His actions so scandalize his mother that she feels compelled to leave their home. Yet she has already ensured that some part of her own values have in fact been transmitted and will resurface at a later time. At the very moment of parting he recalls his memory of her praying daily before the household shrine and is so saddened that he would not see her there any more that he is moved to tears. Every night of his boyhood, waiting for his father, he had listened to her stories of Devaka "... a hero, saint, or something of the kind" (19). Later on in his chequered career as he assumes the role of holy man he impresses his first disciple with "'Do you know the story?' He started narrating the story of Devaka. . ." (17). The decision is explicitly made by his father not to send the boy to the local Albert Mission School because "it seems they try to convert our boys into Christians and are all the time insulting our gods" (23).

If social changes and the corruption of the town have created the rogue, his removal to the village where the traditional pieties still remain appears to purge him of confusion. Narayan's protagonist ultimately shows a capacity for spiritual survival which is related to the still lingering configurations of traditional forces. It could be held that Narayan's novel portrays a more optimistic vision of a society changed perhaps but not destroyed by the experiences of colonialism and modernization. Achebe's portrayal of a protagonist more nearly submerged in the rottenness of the "fat-dripping, gummy, eat-and-let-eat regime just ended" (167) appears more deeply pessimistic. Achebe achieves here in one sense his declared aim in writing, of helping his people "to look back and try and find out where we went wrong" (*Morning* 44). In any case in the wisdom and clarity of his portrayal, the poised detachment of his interpretation of facets of the experience of his people there is a continuing invitation to understanding and therefore cause for hope.

Authorial Ideology and Narrative Technique in *A Man of the People*

DHRUBA GUPTA

"During the earliest stage, critics were engaged in the futile exercise of appointing literary godfathers for African writers—Chinua Achebe drew on Hardy; J.P. Clark on Hopkins; Okigbo on Ezra Pound—and attempted to judge the new literature by the motivation and orientation of the old. This type of criticism was not helpful to the development of African literature, and the less said about it, the better" (Taiwo xiii). A South Asian reader would unavoidably share this indignation with Taiwo, having also had to tolerate judgements of a similar nature: Bankimchandra Chatterjee was hailed as Bengal's Scott, Tagore as Bengal's Shelley, and the novelist Saratchandra Chatterjee likened to Charles Dickens. Things may appear to have improved since the political demise of colonialism, but even now, the glossy back cover of a paperback edition of *Wedding Song* by Egypt's Nobel laureate novelist Naguib Mahfouz contains this illuminating statement from an essay by Edward Said in the *London Review of Books:* "He [Mahfouz] is not only a Hugo and a Dickens, but also a Galsworthy, a Mann, a Zola and Jules Romain" (10). One has to wonder what crime prevents the inclusion of other luminaries of West European literature in Said's list! Jokes apart, hegemonical control over evaluation of literature from the "Third World" (itself a rather derogatory label) continues at both subtle and vulgar levels. Sunday O. Anozie in his strenuous attempts at applying structuralist models to African poetry, imposes upon it a concept born out of a particular intellectual climate in France and in the USA in the sixties, under the assumption that the structuralists have unearthed the scientific principles that describe an "African Mind" (105-25). Appiah protests against this kind of assessment of African literature by fiercely challenging the pet stereotype of many a social anthropologist that no African community ever possessed a sense of the future, and points out that "there are hundreds of African languages with their associated conceptual systems" (144)—a fact which, therefore, precludes the imposition of a concept generated in Paris.

The other side of the picture is also of little help to the South Asian reader in his attempt to approach a modern Nigerian text. As a reaction to Eurocentrism, the reader is often asked to consider African literature from an "African" aesthetic point of view, without any clear indication of what such "Africanness" really means, other than to examine modern African literature in relation to the precolonial oral traditions of different communities. But one can hardly ignore that the "power of event"—to borrow a term that Achebe uses in a somewhat different context (Jeyifo 12)—has considerably changed the African psyche (I do not refer, here, to the "essential" immutable African Mind, for I do not care to venture into the metaphysical) and that as a consequence a new identity has emerged which must strive for new modes of expression to give vent to new feelings and ideas.

From Wole Soyinka's tirade against critics, both European (Gerald Moore, Bernth Lindfors) and African (Jeyifo), it may appear that he believes that new modes of expression should be guided neither by what he calls leftocracy (based on a superficial application of Marxist concepts) nor by prescriptive norms from the West ("The Critic and Society" 27-57). He is most sarcastic about the idea of "Africanness" as a vogue. But his own attitude suffers from a kind of indefiniteness prompted by his own ideology: he seems to believe in what he himself calls a "revolutionary humanism," irrespective of when and where the humanist is situated. The concept of universal humanism gives backbone to a strong plea by both Soyinka and Achebe to continue writing in English. The Indian reader is bound to be troubled by this statement, since modern Indian literatures have always been written in Indian languages (which no one in his right mind would brand as "ethnic dialects"); in contrast, modern African literature is written largely in English, French and Portugese (for obvious reasons, I exclude North Africa). Bengali prose did not exist as a means of meaningful literary expression before the nineteenth century, but was created against the "power of events" by enlightened individuals such as Ram Mohan Roy, Vidyasagar, Bankimchandra Chatterjee, Madhusudan Datta, and more recently, Rabindranath Tagore. Both Bankimchandra and Madhusudan began their literary careers by writing in English, but soon were disenchanted and realized that they would have to write in their own language, even create it or rather mould it to their needs, if they were truly to be "men of their people." The problems of self-expression in a foreign language thus encouraged them to develop indigenous modern literature.

It may well be that Soyinka and Achebe can "speak, think and dream" in English, as the young Madhusudan had wanted to (advising all educated Bengalees to follow suit), but does this not pose a problem in our attempts at defining the "Africanness" of modern African literature? Particularly perplexing is Soyinka's suggestion, in his preface to the Methuen edition of his *Six Plays*, that Swahili, a language whose domain extends little beyond the boundaries of East Africa, be accepted as a lingua franca for the entire African continent (xx). At the opposite pole, of course, are those who doubt the "Africanness" of Swahili altogether. But equally disturbing is Achebe's prescription that English be used in Nigeria for "national" literature and the regional languages for "ethnic" literature only (*Morning* 55-62). A Bengali reader would find it hard to endure the notion of works by Tagore or Bibhutibhusan Banerjee being composed in English, rather than in "ethnic" Bengali, so that they might have wider audience. Translation might serve to reconcile "regionality" and "internationality," but translation is bound to convey less than the original; nonetheless, as a kind of passport to a foreign reality, it remains the only viable solution. Consider, in this context, the recent works written in and translated into indigenous African languages by Ngugi wa Thiong'o of Kenya and Ousmane Sembene of Senegal. Achebe and Soyinka, on the other hand, have resisted expressing themselves in African languages, for reasons entirely their own.

* * *

The question of language choice has been emphasised because Achebe in addresses and interviews has stated that he wishes to remain a "teacher" to his readers (*Morning* 42-45). One may ask, whom does he desire to teach? Is it the English-speaking people as a whole, the English-speaking people of his continent, or primarily those of his own country? I would imagine that when he thinks of himself as an author-teacher, he has in mind his own people as his target audience. Someone who intends to teach not just a craft but also social values is bound to be guided by an ideology, and that ideology must be a product partly of the "power of events" and partly of the author's subjectivity. In Terry Eagleton's terms, his AuI (Authorial Ideology) is closely related to the prevalent GMP (General Mode of Production), LMP (Literary Mode of Production), GI (General Ideology) and AI (Aesthetic Ideology) (44). In simpler terms, Achebe's intention was a product of the interaction of the historical forces of his time with the general aesthetic constructs in his region and the prevalent political atmosphere. "Ideology," in this connection, is not used in a negative sense but rather as indicating the particular intentionality of an author, an intentionality which has roots in his historical situation and reveals his desire, as a subject, to mould and reshape that situation, through the indirect means of literature, in accordance with his consciousness and conscience. This intentionality has been expressed with utmost clarity by Ngugi wa Thiong'o in the following lines:

> the product of a writer's pen both reflects reality and also attempts to persuade us to take a certain attitude to that reality. The persuasion can be a direct appeal on behalf of a writer's open doctrine or it can be an indirect appeal through 'influencing the imagination, feelings and actions of the recipient' in a certain way toward a certain goal and a set of values, consciously or unconsciously held by him (*Writers in Politics* 7).

Contrary to what many critics believe, this intentionality of the author is not at odds with the sheer urge for self-expression, an urge which seems to be truly universal. The perception of an inherent contradiction between the psychological factor of self-expression and the social factor of persuasion through communication, can only be a product of political monomania. In a recent interview with Biodun Jeyifo, Achebe talks of the relationship between the two modes, and his remarks offer a clear picture of the present state of his ideology: (a) The desire to create, he says, is "more like an urge to express yourself . . . self expression, which is a human thing" (3); (b) "Our failure as a nation is a failure of the imagination." So the novelist is to teach readers how to imagine: "one is cruel because one is not imaginative enough . . . a really imaginative person cannot be evil" (14-15); (c) "But [Nigeria] is my country and since . . . providence put me here, my role is to make this place more habitable than I met it. That's our role, that's the role of every generation and that's what civilization is about" (18). As in many of his earlier interviews and speeches, Achebe stresses the role of the writer as a teacher of his people. But for an Indian reader, it remains difficult to understand how Achebe can hope to fulfil such a role if he continues to write exclusively in English. Addressing this generation indirectly, Achebe goes on to say: "Whether you are writing in one language or another, these are not really basic issues, they are important but your soul as an artist cannot be something which you are tinkering with along the way'' (16). Is AuI then a direct and exclusive product of GMP?

*   *   *

Immediately after independence, at a critical juncture of Nigerian history, Achebe felt the need to stand against the ''power of events'' which had shaped his choice of language by writing a highly critical political novel. The bitterness we find in *A Man of the People* is unmistakably an impact of the huge disillusionment that followed the coming of independence in 1960, a glorious year for Nigeria. The bitterness he experienced evidently ushered in a change in the mood and technique of writing, marking a break with the earlier genre of gentle tragedy found in his African Trilogy. The very publication of *A Man of the People* invalidates Abiola Irele's statement: ''Achebe has chosen the tragic medium in handling his theme—as opposed to the comic treatment of the same or similar theme in Oyono and Beti's novels'' (24). By no stretch of the imagination could one say that the ''fall'' of either Chief Nanga or his ''rival'' Odili is a ''tragic'' one, and the theme of the novel is unmistakably comical, making it a seminal text for dark comedy in modern African literature. There is hardly any trace of the urge to establish the ''noble dignity'' of Africa's past in this satirical piece. Kolawole Ogungbesan rightly observes, ''Here he has forsaken his earlier duty to give back to his people their dignity. Now he focusses his gaze on the evils inflicted on the African societies, not by an alien race, but by the Africans themselves'' (46).

In this opus, Chinua Achebe has deliberately used satire in indicting a situation that Soyinka portrays in his excellent novel, *The Interpreters*: ''next to death . . . shit is the most vernacular atmosphere of our beloved country'' (108). But the vexed question of continuity and absorption of African ''tradition'' is raised again in this new context by Barney Charles McCartney in his unpublished Ph.D. thesis when he attempts to make the point that Achebe's satire lacks the traditional motive of amusement and becomes more corrective in its intention, thus becoming more "Western." I see no validity in McCartney's claim that traditional African satire was much less motivated towards social engineering than the so-called "Western" mode of satire from which Achebe allegedly took lessons in planning the text for *A Man of the People*. In fact, there is no valid ground for accepting an invariable binary opposition between "amusement" and social criticism, just as there is no reason to believe that a satirist ceases to be a "teacher," as Adrian Roscoe (129) would have us believe. Consider Aristophanes, whose comedy *The Frogs* was intended both to amuse and advise.

The "non-Africanness" Of *A Man of the People* has been assessed by Roscoe and Lindfors from another perspective: that of the comparative absence of Igbo proverbs. But the conscious use of proverbs by a modern author in a novel should be examined in its particular context. In *Arrow of God,* the proverbs cited are signifiers of the dignity that permeated traditional society, while in *A Man of the People,* the proverbs, along with the pidgin English, have been manipulated by the author to generate a comic effect, except on the rare occasions that involve Odili's father. After all, Achebe did not write his novels to illustrate the theories of any particular school of criticism, but mainly to react to his immediate reality, a reaction he reinforces most eloquently in numerous speeches and interviews. And thus, despite the narrative twist in the middle of *A Man of the People* that tends to give the text the shape of a "posterior retrospection," the novel remains an instant reaction to the palpable reality of the author's present, a depressing present; it is in no way a retrospection, either in anger or in hope. *A Man of the People* is not a contemplative novel, but an instant outburst against the present, both in anger and despair; its sardonic tone distinguishes it from the sad and serene tragedy of *Arrow of God.* Achebe, however, denies the element of "despair" in an interview with Serumaga: "*A Man of the People* is rather a serious indictment—if you like—of post-independence Africa.

But I don't give up because I think this is a necessary stage in our growth'' (Pieterse and Duerden 13). Whether the political turmoil in Nigeria that culminated in Ironsi's 1966 military coup was a ''necessary step'' towards Nigerian and African growth is a difficult question well beyond the scope of this discussion, but that the literary text itself definitely generates a mood of despair, which neither Mad Max's death nor the stand taken by Odili's father succeed in dispelling, is, I feel, incontrovertible. One must admit, however, that a portrait of intense despair, which is not mechanically blessed with an optimistic ''solution,'' can prove quite positive in its long-term effect, if the text is a powerful enough exposition of the elements responsible for despair. ''Creative Pessimism'' is a useful instrument in any indictment of corruption.

That *A Man of the People* was a significant departure from Achebe's earlier works has been noted by several critics who ascribe the change to the writer's moral obligation to react to the altered political situation. Agovi has observed that right from the start, ''The reader's attitude is being manipulated against Nanga'' (191), the archetype of the reactionary generation in power. He posits that in *A Man of the People,* ''the stress is on individualism, and the pursuit of materialism which have brought corruption, strife, cynicism'' (193). But this strong association between the listed vices and ''individualism'' does not wholly characterize the texture of the novel: Nanga's story is not simply that of a man's individual greed. Odili concludes that ''A man's cup might be full and none be the wiser [an example of the conscious modern appropriation of a traditional proverb]. But here the owner knew, and the owner, I discovered, is the will of the whole people'' (96). While this technique of post-mortem realization has given the narrative, to a certain extent, a new character, it also demonstrates that the satirist is not blaming individual greed so much as the failure of the nation as a whole. To David Cook ''it is evident that in *A Man of the People* Achebe is doing something new. He is exploring the situation in a modern African state which is in the process of breaking completely with the past; and the result is that the country enters the age of the isolated individual confronting a mechanical administration, such as we have been deploring in the company of certain European novelists, the most important difference being that in *A Man of the People* this is a new situation, which is just dawning on the protagonist, not an inherited problem to be taken more or less for granted'' (21). However, neither Achebe nor his many critics (except in passing references to the difference between the national movement in Nigeria and the people's struggle in South Africa) address the imperfections and limitations of the anti-colonial national movement itself, which plays an important role, alongside colonial rule itself, in shaping both adversaries, Nanga and Odili, one at the ''possessing'' end and the other at the ''receiving'' end of the ''national cake,'' as it were. Without such an awareness, any instant indictment of pre-independence Nigeria could prove evasive, intellectual, journalistic in a populist manner. The novel neither delves meaningfully into the past, nor envisages a constructive future, contrary to some critics' attention to the so-called ''prophetic'' nature of the text, in view of its publication before Ironsi's coup. The instant reaction of the ''protagonist,'' Cook's ''isolated individual,'' is neither analytical nor predictive.

* * *

Much has been said about the narrative use of the first person singular which obviously gives *A Man of the People* a shape not found in Achebe's previous novels. Roscoe observes, ''Equally important, it also marks a new departure in technique, for Achebe uses here for the first time (and probably in imitation of Mongo Beti), a *persona*, a mouthpiece or other-self, who can conveniently and independently narrate and comment on the events of the plot'' (129). Bergson maintains that somebody who wants to laugh at something must dissociate himself from that thing itself; a satirist is always an outsider in one way or another (62-64). This distancing must be examined in the context of the degree to which the narrator is a mouthpiece of the author. In *A Man of the People* the use of the first person appears to some extent to be inconsistent and unsatisfactory. Up to Chapter Five, the narrator is the spokesman of the author, a representative of the wronged revealing the wrongdoer. Abruptly from Chapter Six, the first person begins to engage in a kind of self-analysis, elaborating on the narrator's personal past, previously discussed in terse code in Chapter Three, and then finally preparing himself, rather comically, to seek revenge on the wrongdoer, both politically and sexually. One could perhaps say that up to Chapter Five, the author identifies himself totally with the first person in order to ridicule the corrupt "unimaginative" power structure symbolized by Nanga, and then suddenly dissociates himself from the first person in order to portray the comical fate of the first person himself; the critic thus becomes an object of criticism for the creator of the critic. This sharp diversion in such a terse narrative sits uneasy, however, with the reader.

It has been claimed that Achebe balances the "evil" aspects of Nanga's character by including certain positive elements such as his "charming" personality, his urge to share the "national cake" with Odili, our "relatively detached observer . . . outside the political reward system" (Wren 99). Such analyses represent the conventional attitude towards character assessment, where each individual must combine "good" and "evil." In fact, Achebe does not portray Nanga as a "character" at all, but purely as a signifier of corruption, a target; he is "one of the finest rogues in Nigerian literature" (Lindfors 15). Achebe adds the psychological finery not to make the character wholesome or convincing, but as a device for making the satire more pungent. Unfortunately, however, in its excessive use of a familiar stereotype, the satire itself panders to the general populist level of social criticism, particularly in the frequent digs at Nanga's horrendous English, his crude jokes, his granting of permission to white men to address him by his first name. his bracketing of

Michael West and Dudley Stamp with High Literature, his assertion that a live man was a victim of a "fatal accident," his pathological hatred for Higher Education, his demand for "constructive criticism" only from people like Jalio, who is condescendingly labelled "a well comported young man" (76). The familiarity of these devices detracts from the mordancy of the satire, as it does, sadly enough, in Wole Soyinka's *A Play of Giants* where he uses the same tired devices to indict African military dictatorships that have flourished under the protection of World Powers. Had Achebe succeeded in releasing himself from the confines of realism with a little more indulgence and "imagination" and made his comedy more "absurd," his indictment would have been more powerful.

The comedy that surrounds the narrator, the representative of the wronged, once he has shed his role as mouthpiece, also seems to lack force, for the self-analysis and self-realization are shrouded in self-pity. The conflation of sexual and political revenge is neither sufficiently amusing nor sufficiently pathetic. A seemingly conscientious intellectual who at the beginning "had felt, like so many other educated citizens of our country, that things were going seriously wrong without being able to say just how" (44), and who then, suddenly decides to reveal the cowardice that ultimately leads to his failure and (I will maintain) despair, presents an extremely unconvincing "I," which fervent admirers of the text hail as its "complexity." Barthold's claim that Odili, who thought long afterward that the modern "owner" of the "cup" of the old proverb was the "will of the people" and not just the individual, and who thereby reached "a degree of self-awareness and clear perception and implication of what he sees around it" (29) is not substantiated by the text. This so-called "clear perception" is hardly integral to the text but occurs almost as an afterthought, encapsulated in a few postscript sentences. In the final analysis, such conscious narrative introspection appears too scanty for the reality that Achebe seeks to portray.

* * *

Doris Lessing, in her introduction to *The Golden Notebook*, says "And when a book's pattern and the shape of its inner life is as plain to the reader as it is to the author—then perhaps it is time to throw the book aside, as having had its day, and start again on something new" (xxiv). Though it would be preposterous to suggest that *A Man of the People* has had its day and ought now to be "thrown away," Lessing's judgement on her own creation gives a kind of support to my candid admission that a second reading of Achebe's novel after a gap of twenty-four years, makes me less enthusiastic about its success as a work of literature than I was upon my first encounter. The novel now seems to resolve into two separate works, both blueprints rather than complete structures, the first ending with Chapter Six. Certain contemplations of Odili, such as "I thought much afterwards" (97) and "I thought to myself: You do not belong to this age, old man. Men of worth nowadays simply forget what they said yesterday" (152) may appear to unite the whole narrative into a flashback, but this does not save it from its essential lack of integration. Furthermore, this justification of the narrative raises the question of why the device of reminiscence is used in the first place. Is Odili narrating his story to achieve some sort of personal catharsis, or does he attempt, at the same time, to "teach" his audience some important lessons of life? Such supratextual questions can hardly be avoided in examining a novel that intends not only to "amuse" but also to "advise."

Yet, although in the ultimate analysis one is tempted to conclude that Achebe is far more in his element in the province of tragedy, as evidenced by *Arrow of God*, his attempts at comedy remain immensely valuable as examples of Literary Mode of Production (LMP) conditioned by Authorial Ideology (AuI) as both in *A Man of the People* and in *Anthills of the Savannah*, Achebe proves himself to be a glorious keeper of conscience, a writer genuinely concerned with the destiny of his people during a very troubled period in his nation, his continent, and the world as a whole.

Beyond Ideology: Achebe's Political Vision in *Anthills of the Savannah*

GOVIND NARAIN SHARMA

Achebe's *Anthills of the Savannah* is a political novel about Nigeria, a "crazy log-book of this our ship of state"; a clinical report which is an outcome of the narrator's "disenchantment . . . turned long ago into detached clinical interest" (2). However, it is much more than merely a disinterested diagnosis of the malady afflicting the Nigerian state: neither the author nor the narrators are really "detached." All of them have a passionate concern for their country. The novel, therefore, also offers a prescription for curing the malady, for restoring the nation to health and vitality. What is most striking about Achebe's approach to the entire problem and what places him in sharp contrast to most of the other leading African writers and thinkers such as La Guma, Ousmane, Ngugi, Soyinka, Armah, Fanon and Cabral is his unconcealed antipathy to ideology of every kind.

While trying to understand Achebe's antipathy to ideology, I would like to suggest in this essay that it is impossible for a writer not to have an ideology, that with all his suspicion of and antagonism to ideology, Achebe does have an ideology of his own, and that the "new radicalism" he advocates is really a form of philosophic conservatism which has remarkable similarities to the thought of conservative thinkers such as Burke, Coleridge, Disraeli and Arnold from England and Gandhi from India. However, this conservatism, based as it is on an idealistic interpretation of reality and history, is incapable either of understanding the forces which operate in the international arena today or coping with the problems of modern post-industrial societies. I would also like to consider whether Achebe's antipathy to ideology is misplaced and whether, in spite of the genuineness of his concern, it limits, compromises and confuses his position as a social critic.

I

Ideology is a much-misunderstood term and we might clarify the sense in which we are going to use it. Though the word ideology was first coined by the French philosopher Desutt de Tracy at the end of the eighteenth century, it is the left Hegelians who gave it its significance as a way of translating ideas into action. However, it is with Marx that the term acquired its current importance. Ideology, in the Marxist sense, has been defined as "the sum of conceptions which enables a social group (a social class, for example, but not only a class) to systematize the *values* in which the mystified consciousness and the activity of this group are expressed" (Kolakowski in Bottomore 119). Ideology is thus an artificial construct divorced from the material conditions of a people's existence, and its function is to legitimize the power of the ruling class in society, for in the last analysis the dominant ideas of a society are the ideas of its ruling class. Historical materialism is, in this sense, not an ideology. As Terry Eagleton observes, it "stands or falls by the claim that it is not only not an ideology, but that it contains a scientific theory of the genesis, structure and decline of ideologies" (16). It was not much later, in Stalin's time as Kolakowski points out, that Marxists themselves came to use "ideology" to denote "all forms of social consciousness, including those that were supposed to present a scientific account of the world, free from mystification and distortion" (154). The distinction in the minds of Marxists has been that historical materialism is true ideology or "science" while others such as bourgeois economics, politics, law and religion are false ideologies. I propose to apply the term "ideology" to both Marxism as well as to other systems of ideas and representations which dominate the mind of a man or of a social group, which are used by them to interpret or explain reality, to make sense of the world.

II

Achebe's dissatisfaction with ideology stems from his experience of Nigerian politics and society during the last thirty years and manifests itself in three forms—dissatisfaction with the situation in Nigeria and with the behaviour of the leftists in particular; with leftist ideology as reflected in the behaviour of leftists in Africa as a whole; and with ideology in general. Politics in Nigeria, he notes in *Anthills*, has no relation to "the lives and concerns of ninety-nine percent of the population" (141). The term "public affairs" is a misnomer, for it refers to "nothing but the closed transactions of soldiers-turned-politicians with their cohorts in business and the bureaucracy" (141). Conditions in Nigeria are, however, not an exception: they are representative of those in Africa as a whole. Moreover, it is not the soldier-politicians, businessmen and bureaucrats alone who are corrupt. Those who claim to represent the progressive forces in society—leaders of the proletariat such as trade unionists, left-wing intellectuals such as university professors and leaders of student unions—are all equally selfish, corrupt and unprincipled, which makes them "in the real context of Africa today . . . not the party of the oppressed but of the oppressor" (159). The main attribute of the "new radicalism" Achebe's fictional surrogate in the novel Ikem Osodi expounds would be that "first and foremost, [it] must be clear-eyed enough to see beyond the present claptrap that will heap all our problems on the doorstep of capitalism and imperialism" (158). It is, in his opinion, "sheer cant and humbug" to blame all the evils of their society on "imperialism and international capitalism" (159).

Achebe's disillusionment with ideology should not, however, be viewed as a peculiarly African phenomenon but a more universal one. It represents in part the disillusionment of the liberal intellectual who had been nurtured on the dreams of Progress and Perfectibility for two hundred years since the Enlightenment and the French Revolution in the wake of the economic depression of the 30s and the 40s, the rise of fascism, the holocaust and the carnage of the two imperialistic World Wars. It is an important strain in the literature of Modernism such as the writings of Eliot, Joyce and Yeats, authors whom Achebe holds in esteem and from whom he has borrowed the titles of two of his novels. But in the case of Achebe there is another dimension too. His disillusionment is in substantial measure that of the Third World intellectual who had pinned great hopes on the process of de-colonization which began with the independence of India in 1947 and culminated with that of most of the countries of Asia and Africa by the early sixties. Since imperialism and colonialism had been regarded as the root cause of their problems, it was hoped that a new era of peace and prosperity—a *Ram-Rajya* (reign of Rama, the incarnation of God according to the Hindus) as Gandhi visualized it—would begin with independence. These hopes were, however, soon shattered, and *Anthills of the Savannah*, in its portrayal of postcolonial disillusionment, is in the same category of novels as Peter Abrahams's *A Wreath for Udomo*, Armah's *The Beautyful Ones Are Not Yet Born,* Ngugi's *Petals of Blood,* Rushdie's *Midnight's Children* and Achebe's own *A Man of the People.* What singles out *Anthills of the Savannah* is Achebe's fierce onslaught on ideology, and his angry reminder that it has been exploited by interested parties for hoodwinking the people by blaming the problems of the nation on foreigners, thus covering up their own crimes and sins.

Achebe's contemptuous dismissal of ideology does not, however, make him free from ideology. As Louis Althusser has remarked, "man is an ideological animal by nature" (160); "ideology slides into all human activity, . . . it is identical with the 'lived' experience of human existence itself" (204). Since the artist is a human being, he must have an ideology. "The peculiarity of art," according to Althusser, "is to 'make us see' (*nous donner a voir*), 'make us perceive', 'make us feel' something which alludes to reality." "What art makes us *see*, and therefore gives to us in the form of 'seeing', 'perceiving' and 'feeling' (which is not the form of *knowing*), is the *ideology* from which it is born, in which it bathes, from which it detaches itself as art, and to which it *alludes*." As Pierre Macherey has shown in the case of Tolstoy, by extending Lenin's analyses, and as Althusser shows in the case of Balzac and Solzhenitsyn, these writers give us "a view of ideology to which their work alludes and with which it is constantly fed, a view which presupposes a *retreat*, an *internal distantiation* from the very ideology from which their novels emerged. They make us 'perceive' (but not know) in some sense *from the inside*, by an *internal distance* the very ideology in which they are held" (204).

We see a similar process of distantiation at work in *Anthills of the Savannah*. It would, therefore, be worthwhile discovering the ideology from which Achebe's novel has emerged, in which it is held. The plot of the novel hinges on the willingness of His Excellency the President of the country to visit Abazon, the distant north-western region which has been in the grip of a severe drought for the last two years and where the people have been going through great suffering. This willingness is the litmus test of the sensitivity of the elite to the problems of the people, of whether the rulers are willing to identify themselves with the people, or, like their former colonial masters, they are more obsessed with questions of their own dignity and status as shown in their determination to keep their distance from the rabble. They choose the latter course because, in their view, it is only distance which can protect the mystique of power, something absolutely vital for maintaining law and order in the country. In nothing else perhaps is the Western orientation of the ruling elite more clearly reflected than in this belief: that is how their colonial masters had preserved their power and glory and this is what their successors are determined to do. The present President is also annoyed with the Abazonians because they did not support him in the referendum for life presidency, but the contempt for the mass of the people is the main reason for his refusal to visit them or to listen to their grievances.

The characters in the novel are easily divided into the good guys and the bad guys: those who support closer contact with the people, are sympathetic to their problems and responsive to their needs are good; those who are lacking in these virtues or opposed to this approach are bad. Invariably, the latter are Western in their orientation, and His Excellency furnishes the most glaring example. Like Chris and Ikem, Sam was a product of Lord Lugard College in Nigeria. However, it was his training at Sandhurst and his stay in England which was the strongest formative influence on his personality. He admired the English "to the point of foolishness" and "his major flaw was that all he ever wanted was to do what was expected of him especially by the English" (49)—as well as by the Americans, for one of his nightmares was to appear on "the cover of *Time* magazine with a big mouth and a small head" (15). No wonder the visit of the six-man Abazon delegation to Bassa should remind H.E. of the Israeli raid on Entebbe airport in Uganda (15).

Achebe's political creed seems to be a radical form of populism, but it would be more enlightening to see it as belonging to a richer and more venerable tradition of thought—the tradition of philosophic conservatism represented by Burke, Coleridge, Disraeli, Arnold and Gandhi. And there is a remarkable similarity between the political, social and intellectual circumstances in which Achebe's own political views and these traditions developed. Burke's conservatism in *Reflections on the Revolution in France* was articulated as a response to the reason-intoxicated thought of the French and English radicals who based their claims for freedom and equality on metaphysical speculation, or what is called ideology today. As opposed to abstract concepts such as natural rights, Burke put forward the claims of experience and history, "the general sense of mankind," the wisdom of the race, stemming from the conviction that the individual is foolish . . . but the species is wise." By despising everything that belonged to us, as he declared, we would be setting up our "trade without a capital" (122). Arnold's definition of culture "as the best that is known and thought in the world" in *Culture and Anarchy* (xviii) is only another name for the accumulated experience of mankind which is represented in society in the form of individuals as well as institutions. Those who set themselves against these repositories of the wisdom of the race—as the Nonconformists did in their hostility to the Church of England—isolate themselves from "the main current of national life," and thus deliberately turn their faces against the most powerful agencies of civilization and culture.

Achebe's objection to ideologies and systems is on similar grounds. These are mostly abstract concepts— "metaphysical speculation"—which do not make any allowance for the history and culture of a nation. They suffer from another shortcoming in relation to Africa: they have been developed following the observation of and in response to social, economic and political conditions totally different from those prevailing in Africa. The great shortcoming of "the present orthodoxies of deliverance" is that they fail to perceive local differences, to recognize the "peculiar hell that the oppressed inhabit" (*Anthills* 99). They also fail to take into account the complexity of human nature: "The simplistic remedies touted by all manner of salesmen (including some who call themselves artists) will always fail because of man's stubborn antibody called surprise. Man will surprise by his capacity for nobility as well as for villainy. No system can change that. It is built into the core of man's free spirit" (99). Achebe, like Burke, is opposed to revolution, for while revolution might be necessary under exceptional circumstances "for taking society out of an intractable stretch of quagmire . . . it does not confer freedom, and may indeed hinder it" (99). Achebe, therefore, like Burke, is committed to a philosophy of gradualism—to reform rather than revolution, relying, as Burke did, more on experience than theory: "Experience and intelligence warn us that man's progress in freedom will be piecemeal, slow and undramatic" (99).

Achebe is not opposed to change; neither was Burke. Change, however, should be in accordance with tradition, or what Burke would call "inheritance." The idea of inheritance, as he says, "furnishes a sure principle of conservation, and a sure principle of improvement. It leaves acquisition free, but it secures what it acquires" (120). Achebe's Ikem Osodi ridicules Marxist systems such as dictatorship of the proletariat because, in them, "roots have already been dug up and branches hacked away" (139). The importance Achebe attaches to roots and branches is shown in the organic imagery he employs, revealing a striking affinity with Burke and other conservative thinkers in their pronounced preference for what has grown to what has been made. Standing out in his *Reflections* is the magnificent simile in which Burke compares the English constitution to the British oak and the people of England to the great cattle silently chewing the cud. It was possible that the political wisdom of the English people manifested in their quiet and contented existence under the protective shade of the British oak might be overlooked and their silence be drowned out by the shrill sloganeering of the small bunch of radicals— "the half a dozen grasshoppers under a fern [which] make the field ring with their importunate chink" (97). Achebe seems to have a similar apprehension. "The young tree planted by David Diop on the edge of the primeval desert" (139) represents, like Burke's oak, the indigenous accumulated wisdom of the African people rooted in experience and history. This alone, not the borrowed and half-baked theories of leftist African radicals, can provide direction for the future growth of African nations and societies. The experience of the race is embedded not so much in our intellect as in our instincts, not in our conscious but in our subconscious mind and, on finding a suitable stimulus, can sprout forth just as Ikem's awareness "going far, far back in his subconscious mind waiting like a dormant seed in the dry season soil for the green-fingered magician, the first rain" was triggered by the visit of the men of the people, the taxi-drivers (140).

The most significant instance of organic imagery, however, is the one contained in the title of the novel. The master-symbol of the tale, the anthills, which survive "to tell the new grass of the savannah about last year's brush fires"(31) are the venerable elders of Abazon who are the embodiments of the accumulated experience of the community, the instinctive wisdom of the race. They have passed through many ups and downs, have seen several ambitious politicians and dictators such as His Excellency come and go without having their composure shaken. They will survive the current crisis too to tell the coming generations— "the new grass"—about the coups and countercoups— "last year's brush fires"—and not to be upset by them unduly but carry on the task of ordering their lives and building the nation.

IV

Achebe thus does have an ideology. It is an ideology which decries an excessive reliance on reason and logic—Ikem's convictions are based more on intuition than logic (140)—and places more faith in instinct and intuition, experience and history, and looks for the hidden wisdom that is contained in myth. But myth itself is a form of ideology, a "*concrete systematization of values;* that is, an assemblage of values which are embodied not in abstractions, but in particular individuals and situations, and which serve to unify the social group which generated them" (Kolakowski in Bottomore 120). While deriding the ideologies of others as "majestic visions of transforming the world" which are nothing more than "grand illusions," Achebe develops his own "majestic vision" in the form of the myth of an organic society, based on a union of the elite and the people and undisturbed by unsettling notions such as the conflict of classes. Achebe does recognize a cleavage in the body-politic. However, this cleavage is not between the bourgeoisie and the proletariat: it is between the poor, illiterate peasant mass and the affluent, educated and Westernized elite who have nothing but contempt for the former. The four "angels" in the novel—Ikem, Chris, Beatrice and Emmanuel—all make heroic efforts to bridge this gap. Ikem "marries" Elewa, a true daughter of the people, even boasting to the students that his "prospective mother-in-law sells tie-die cloth in Gelegele market" and so "qualifies along with peasants for a seat among the proletariat" (156-57). Emmanuel courts Edamma; Beatrice, who is so high and mighty with servants such as Agatha in the beginning, goes through her "conversion" and learns to be nice, not merely to Agatha and to Elewa, but to Elewa's mother and her hard-drinking uncle, the medicine-man. Chris does not exactly develop an amorous interest in a daughter of the people—for the high-minded and sophisticated "priestess of the unknown god" (224) Beatrice could hardly be relegated to such an ordinary status. But he does something even nobler: he sacrifices himself protecting the honour of one from the bestial onslaught of an instrument of brutal militarism, thus proving himself a "gentleman" in the true English sense of the word.

The exemplary behaviour of Ikem, Chris, Beatrice and Emmanuel is meant as an object lesson to Nigerians. Achebe's solution to the problem of the cleavage of classes recalls Disraeli's in *Sybil: or The Two Nations* where the marriage of Egremont, a scion of the aristocracy, to Sybil, a daughter of the people, reconciles the Two Nations—the Rich and the Poor—and promotes the ideal of an organic society. It also reminds us of another version of the organic society, the Gandhian, where equality as a social ideal would be quietly forgotten because of its sheer impracticability but justice would be achieved through moral suasion by exhorting the rich to treat their wealth as a trust for the poor. And in the interest of social harmony the virtuous poor would willingly accept the guardianship of the rich.

Achebe's vision of harmony extends further than myth and embraces symbolism, ritual and mysticism. The union of the elite and the people—Ikem and Elewa—brings about a new birth, the baby girl Amaechina—May-the-path-never-close, the

Shining Path of Ikem—symbolizing the new Nigeria, free from social cleavage and bound by the ties of brotherhood and friendship. This is how "the primitive integrity of the earth" (142), which had been violated when her favourite children—the famine-stricken peasantry of Abazon—had been insulted and humiliated, is now restored. Religious cleavage is overcome in the "ecumenical fraternization" (224) of the ritual dance celebrating the birth of the new nation. However, earth is not the only divinity to be appeased: there is also "an alienated [and] embittered history" which carefully programmes in advance the fate of individuals and nations (220) and which has to be propitiated with blood-sacrifice, the blood of angels such as Ikem and Chris.

Achebe's vision of harmony and happiness might seem too optimistic to some, in spite of the deterministic strain in it which we have just noted. We are faced here with two moral and metaphysical conceptions of history and social reality. According to one, exploitation and injustice in the world are the result of human wickedness and folly and can be removed by the moral reformation of the individual, for "society is an extension of the individual" (*Anthills* 99). According to the other view, based on a materialist interpretation of reality, exploitation and injustice are "the effect of laws of social development which make it inevitable that at a certain stage of history one class, pursuing its interests with varying degrees of rationality, should dispossess and exploit another" (Berlin 5). This view assumes a built-in conflict between the rich and the poor, the haves and the have-nots, based on a conspiracy of the rich to rob the poor. Achebe rejects the latter view the and has no patience with those "partisans, patriots and party-liners" who, thinking in terms of class, "would see no blot of villainy in the beloved oppressed nor grant the faintest glimmer of humanity to the hated oppressor" (*Anthills* 100). Change for him does not require any drastic overhauling of social and economic organization such as ownership of the means of production: what is required is the rectification of "a basic human failing that may only be alleviated by a good spread of general political experience" (139). He has a deep-seated trust in the ability of individuals to create new meanings and values which will bring into existence a new social and political order. "The trouble with Nigeria," as he says in the booklet bearing the same title, "is simply and squarely a failure of leadership" (1). His Excellency's kowtowing to American journalists is just a personal weakness, almost a foible, an outcome of his early education and training and his extended stay in Western countries. If the nation had a new leader more deeply rooted in Nigerian culture—Mallam Aminu Kano, for instance—all these problems would not arise. Whether a new leader who was strongly committed to the political and economic independence of the country would not, in pursuing this goal, come into conflict with the forces of international monopoly capitalism in the U.S.A. or with vested interests within the country does not seem to be relevant because to raise these issues is to take recourse to the familiar claptrap of ideology.

It is difficult to avoid the impression that Achebe's allergy to ideology, which as it turns out is mainly to leftist ideology springing largely from his disgust with the behaviour of self-proclaimed revolutionaries in his country and as seen in his exclusively idealistic interpretation of reality, dilutes his social criticism in *Anthills of the Savannah*. It could even be argued that he betrays the same weakness in his social and political thought— "the seminal absence of intellectual rigour" (*The Trouble with Nigeria* 11)—which he deplores in the thought of the founding fathers of the Nigerian nation. The argument would not be fully justified because Achebe, as we have seen, does have an ideology of his own which belongs to a rich and respected tradition—the tradition of philosophic conservatism. Though a bit vague and paternalistic and not adequately equipped to cope with the problems of modern post-industrial societies, it is solidly built on the humanistic virtues of freedom and dignity of the individual. Moreover, Achebe is an artist, not a metaphysician or theorist. His politics, therefore, in the tradition of poets and novelists such as Whitman, Eliot and Yeats, Joyce and Lawrence, is the politics of vision, a vision which, though idealistic and utopian, is at the same time authentically African in its open-hearted generosity, warmth and humanity.

The Story and the Struggle in *Anthills of the Savannah*

SUPRIYA NAIR

The function of art, or more specifically literature, in society is an issue that we find repeatedly addressed in the African literary context. The relationship between the writer and his/her audience, history, social context, race, class, and so on seems particularly important in newly independent societies that face the task of rebuilding the nation and redefining their goals after centuries of colonial domination. Works such as the Kenyan writer Ngugi wa Thiong'o's *Writers in Politics* (1981) clearly locate the socially responsible writer as a political activist who opposes the hegemony of Western imperialism and/or local state authority through literature. "Literature and writers cannot be exempted from the battlefield," asserts Ngugi (73). Through the challenges to traditional, particularly Western, middle class power structures, canonical notions of the function and form of literature as well as the identity and role of the writer are forced to be redefined. What Barbara Harlow calls "Resistance Literature" explodes the generic and thematic preconceptions of literature as a "higher" form of art supposedly universal but beyond the reach of the common audience, especially the lower classes. Harlow includes in her study a wide range of literary forms, including short stories, poems, and prison memoirs emerging out of specific historical conditions of struggle against various forms of domination. The point of this emergent literature is to enable those who have been objectified to reclaim their rightful positions as subjects of history. It also calls for the continuation of struggle as new forms of oppression arise after each revolutionary moment.

Chinua Achebe has always insisted that an African writer cannot afford the luxury of ignoring social issues when so much remains to be done after independence. His most recent collection of essays, *Hopes and Impediments* (1988), reiterates his stand on the social function of the writer/artist. The titles of his essays, some of which had been published earlier, are in themselves revealing: "The Novelist as Teacher," "The Writer and His Community," "What Has Literature Got to Do With It?" are all essays that proclaim the writer's functions of guidance and even leadership in his society. Achebe also disclaims the notion of individualist art since, by his definition, art is both functional and communal and therefore has to meet the needs and demands of the people.

Achebe's fiction has been equally insistent on a connection to his specific political situation. His novels, short stories, and poems have kept pace with the unfolding developments of Nigerian history. His latest novel, *Anthills of the Savannah,* which was published in 1987, is perhaps his most explicit comment on the place and function of literature in the modern Nigerian context. The novel includes various types of literature, ranging from autobiographical accounts and poems to communiques, graffiti, folktales, lectures, and the cryptic sign-writing on buses. All these literary forms speak in different ways to the specific social predicament in Kangan (a fictional military state in Africa that closely resembles modern Nigeria) by telling various stories. The need to tell a story in order to be reminded of the past and to cope with the pressures of the present is an indefatigable natural instinct: "The trees had become hydra-headed bronze statues so ancient that only blunt residual features remained on their faces, like anthills surviving to tell the new grass of the savannah about last year's brush fires" (31). Likewise, the storytelling embodied in literature is not a mere exercise in creativity, but an active expression of the daily struggle to "survive."

A Man of the People (1966), a novel that preceded *Anthills* by two decades, provides the prologue to the later work, ending as it does with a military coup in the wake of widespread corruption, political chaos, and election fraud. Achebe's uncanny foresight regarding the actual Nigerian coup of January 1966 has already been remarked on by various critics and political observers. It calls to mind his own remark on the prophetic role of storytellers "who had the dual role to *foretell* and to *forth-tell*" in order to be fully responsible to their audience (Chametzky 7). In *A Man of the People,* the first-person narrator, Odili Samalu, fails to respond to the needs of the "poor contemptible people" and "silly, ignorant villagers" from whom he separates himself (2). Both Odili and Obi in *No Longer at Ease* (1960) belong to the "hybrid class" of intellectuals who find themselves functioning as intermediaries between the politicians and the people. The "general anti-intellectual feeling" in Odili's state is proof that the intellectuals had aligned themselves with the group in power, neglecting the largely illiterate masses who expected more from these leaders of the future.

A similar contempt for "these half-baked professors" is expressed in *Anthills,* ironically by the President who has been educated in exclusive schools in both Kangan and London. In the tradition of most postcolonial countries, leadership after the coup has been assumed by Western-educated intellectuals, only in this case they come from "the high tradition of proud aloofness from politics and public affairs" (12). So a young Army Commander with virtually no experience in political leadership becomes Head of State, supported by a Cabinet of equally ineffective members divorced from the "outside."

Their position as privileged members of a clique, looking out, as Odili puts it in *A Man of the People,* at the people who have been unable to come in from the rain, is reflected in the stand of the "First Witness" in *Anthills,* Christopher Oriko, Commissioner for Information: "pure, unadulterated disinterest" (4). This cynical and powerless perspective coming from a man who is in charge of national communication speaks for the disenfranchised populace of Kangan. The people's revolution anticipated in the celebrated coups both in Achebe's fiction and Nigerian history has quite unmistakably failed. This failure is reinforced in the novel by the President's refusal to meet the delegation from Abazon and hear their testimony. The story the elders from the northern province have come to tell about the drought in Abazon and their struggle to survive is apparently not important enough for His Excellency's ears. Even the Commissioner for Information does not get to hear it. The only person who hears the entire story is the "Second Witness," Ikem Osodi, a literary artist turned editor of the *National Gazette.* He, in turn, relates it to an audience of more than two thousand students at the University of Bassa in Kangan. His retelling of the elder's narrative is described as "a coup on the audience" who, until this point, are as divorced from the Abazon cause and the problems of the peasants as are their leaders.

Ikem's positioning of the tale in the context of the imprisonment of the elders from Abazon reveals why some stories remain unheard. As he announces to the disturbed audience, "storytellers are a threat" (153). The authenticity of the people's story is a threat to the power structure that places itself outside of and above the people. The act of telling the story is a sign of resistance, a determined attempt to counter official myths of stability and justice with accounts of the Abazonian encounter with the drought. The condition of drought has been aggravated by the President's order to stop boring wells in this recalcitrant "natural guerrilla country," in retaliation for the insult to his position: Abazon alone refuses to "say yes" to the President-for-Life referendum and defeats His Excellency's bid for unlimited authority. The writer's relevance to the power struggle between the periphery and the centre is proved by the elder's acknowledgement that Ikem's silence on the issue had guided their suspicion of the referendum. Not having the approval of the editor, himself a native of Abazon, the villagers realize that Ikem's refusal to speak is a political act conveying his views silently in a state where all speech is carefully monitored.

Ikem's refusal to be silent after his suspension as editor is an equally effective political strategy, especially since the leaders of the delegation from Abazon have been arrested and silenced. Similarly, Chris's reaction after Ikem's death at the hands of the state security forces is to immediately publicize the true account that has been distorted by the state version. The NTBB (Not to Be Broadcast) directive that usually makes Chris's job as Commissioner for Information a farce is effectively countered by the people's irrepressible unofficial broadcasting network, the "VOR, the Voice of Rumour, the despair of tyrants and shady dealers in high places" (168). The right message is as important as the audience it reaches, since it is the force that will direct public response, an eventuality much feared by the increasingly alienated and paranoid President. The destruction of copies of the *National Gazette* by the students because of its distorted representation of Ikem's comment on the President's head is also a recognition of the government's attempt to justify its repressive measures by inventing specious narratives for public consumption. Copies of Chris's account of the actual events that led to Ikem's assassination are instead distributed by the President of the Student's Union, who is then immediately hounded by the state authorities in another effort to suppress threatening information.

The disruption caused by the transmission of information from the writer to the public and the frantic reaction of the government to such "literary guerrillas" demonstrates why storytellers are a threat to the government. Ngugi wa Thiong'o, who frequently uses the above term to indicate the writer's involvement in subversive political activism, was first imprisoned and then exiled after he began writing in Gikuyu for a largely working class and peasant audience. In his prison diary *Detained* (1981), Ngugi exposes the atmosphere of "submission, silence, and obedience" that the Kenyan government imposed on the intellectuals in order to crush opposition to its policies (xi). According to Ngugi, the culture of silence in modern Kenya is a tactic inherited from the colonial power structure. The colonial imperative was based on non-communication, on a denial of the linguistic act. The alternative strategies of whispered messages, sign language, and clandestine reading and writing used by the political detainees are attempts to speak up within the boundaries of the prison walls. The continuing perceptual and linguistic relationships that the detainees seek among themselves and with social realities outside are part of the battle with the prison authorities who try to ensure the virtual entombment of the prisoners by denying them such connections. Ngugi retells the popular fairy tale of the emperor's new clothes, giving it a political reading that situates this "universal" narrative in a specific Kenyan situation: the aversion to hearing a voice that differs from that of the ruling power (179-80). The price of revealing unpalatable and frequently embarrassing realities is heavy, as Ngugi's own experience proves, but the writer has no regrets about his decision to counter enforced silence or masked rhetoric with the "naked" truth. He states his views in *Detained:* "we who write in Kenya, in Africa, in the Third World, are the modern Cassandras of the developing world, condemned to cry the truth against neo-colonialist and imperialist cultures and then be ready to pay for it with incarceration, exile and even death" (191).

The true story is most dangerous when in the hands of the people and so every attempt is made to sever the connection between the writer and the masses. Ngugi's later works, written in Gikuyu, present the workers and peasants as producers of culture rather than as dehumanized objects. His writings stimulated a consciousness of the contributions of the lower classes, especially in their struggle against colonialism, and demanded an increased political participation from the audience. In repressive structures such as those operative in present-day Kenya and Nigeria, "public" information is officially channeled and moulded to allow leadership to maintain power. Lack of information or misleading information keeps the populace ignorant and therefore disempowered, denying them the awareness of political realities necessary for social transformation. Achebe's brief experience of broadcasting in Nigeria seems to have informed his critique of the role that the news media play in a condition of censorship. The reason that the official media in Kangan reports that Ikem is "fatally wounded" rather than baldly states that he has been killed is in the hope that the listening audience will be disarmed by the statement that is usually read as meaning "seriously wounded." Chris's desperate recourse to unofficial channels and foreign media to present his perspective is an ironic comment on the nature of information exchange between the government and the people to whom it is supposed to be responsible.

Given the urgency of the correct message and its delivery into the right hands, Achebe's continual emphasis on the writer's political stance gains significance. In military dictatorships and one-party states, the writer's separation from social realities and distance from his/her particular community would be a blessing to neocolonial hegemony. As seen in the case of Abazon, the writer can actually influence public opinion and check unlimited authority. The writer's refusal, then, to relate to current political issues in the interests of a "universal" literature and a "pure" art results in an aesthetically appealing but functionally sterile "work," an alienated and useless piece of "labour." Achebe's choice is clearly in favour of an unabashedly functional literature, responsible to the writer's community and what he calls "right and just causes," regardless of the interests of those in power (*Morning* 84).

According to Achebe, traditionally, the African artist was free of the dilemma in which he had to choose between a culturally elite art unsullied by popular concerns (and in Nigeria popular concerns are political) or an art that aimed at a wider audience and addressed issues more specific than the inevitable pain of the human condition. In his essay, "The Writer and His Community," Achebe discusses the communal responsibility of the artist, who creates his art in close communion with his people; this demands an identification with their interests and needs (*Hopes and Impediments* 32-41). But in the colonial and neocolonial contexts, the writers have been indoctrinated into a system that allows them the privileges of what Frantz Fanon in *The Wretched of the Earth* calls the "underdeveloped bourgeoisie" the class-in-formation that assumed leadership after independence and inherited and perpetuated colonial structures of inequality. Fanon's prediction of the failure and corruption of this class has materialized into reality, and the proximity of the intellectuals to this class has been a problematic one (121-63). Fanon urges the writers and intellectuals to dissociate themselves from the native petite bourgeoisie that has gained power and align themselves with the lower classes whom he often refers to as "the people."

Achebe's commitment to the powerless groups reveals his dissatisfaction with the ineffective Nigerian middle class and his opposition to the military leadership that has made no attempt to be responsible to the people, but continues the same practices it once condemned in the civilian regime before the series of coups abolished even the pretence of democracy. In an interview with Bernth Lindfors conducted at the University of Texas in 1969, Achebe outlines a double function for the African writer. The first would be as a spokesperson for the presence of a rich African heritage contrary to the colonial myths of a deviant and underdeveloped culture. The second function arises due to the shift in power after independence from white colonialists to black neocolonialists who had too much to gain from the former framework to want to change it. The dismissal of the native Other by the colonizers was repeated by the petit bourgeois leaders who, as represented in *A Man of the People,* ignored the needs of the people and continued to exploit them. 'So I had to become a critic," claims Achebe. "I found myself on the side of the people against their leaders—leaders this time being black people" (Lindfors *et al* 8). Echoing Fanon's own programme for the writers who engage in the process of decolonization, Achebe sees himself reacting to this superficial change in leadership by a shift from his earlier position as cultural historian to that of social critic, a move reflected in the tone and content of his novels. Unlike the passive, distanced position that Chris at first assumes in *Anthills* before the series of explosive events forces a radical transformation, Achebe believes that the writer's place in a social revolution is not near the margins but, as he says in the interview, "right in the thick of it—if possible, at the head of it" (Lindfors *et al* 6). Creativity gains substance and relevance by locating itself and giving voice to the continuing struggle for independence in a different context.

Achebe's double commitment to the past and the present is seen in his use of a third witness in *Anthills*, Beatrice Okoh, Senior Assistant Secretary in the Ministry of Finance, Chris's lover, and Achebe's most articulate female character. Beatrice's autobiographical account, unlike Chris's, stems from an attempt to trace her own weaknesses and check allegations made by people who see her as a power-hungry woman manipulating the men in power. Beatrice's task of "bringing together as many broken pieces of this tragic history" as she can is not an attempt to romanticize her past but to come to grips with the present (82). Achebe's narrative shift to a female voice is his own acknowledgement of the need for female empowerment in the modern African context. The initiative Achebe expects from the African writer is demanded by Beatrice who is tired of being forced, by virtue of her gender, to pick up the spears of defeated men and carry on the battle (91-92). Her reference to Sembene's film critiques the secondary position given to women whose contribution to the liberation struggle has been as much overlooked as that of the working class and peasantry. She therefore chooses her position at the head of the struggle, refusing to claim, however, that her perspective is dominant. Instead, she challenges the male triad of power (Sam, Chris, Ikem) and rebukes Chris's complacency about his position in the hierarchy of power represented by the military leader, cabinet minister, and literary artist: "The story of this country, as far as you are concerned, is the story of the three of you. . ." (66).

Beatrice's dissenting voice in an otherwise male-dominated setting gives her the status of the divine priestess who shares a similar function with the writer in revealing and checking "man's unquenchable thirst to sit in authority on his fellows" (104). The chapter entitled "Daughters: Idemili" focusing on Beatrice's part of the story begins by recalling the traditional ritual involving daughters who are usually neglected in the patriarchal structure. This ritual is based on the myth that when Power ravaged the world, the Sun, the Almighty force, had sent his daughter Idemili to clothe and control Power's naked body. While Beatrice herself is most unaware of native traditions because of her colonial education, she is nevertheless conscious of the role native legends have played in subverting the myths of colonial "history" that justified British rule. As in the story of the bird trilling outside her window, the questioning of "the King's property" has to be continually repeated in order "to bear witness to the moral nature of authority" (102).

Achebe's theoretical works frequently refer to stories that contain cautionary morals about the dangers of seeking excessive power. In an essay, "*Chi* in Igbo Cosmology," he relates the tale of the arrogant wrestler who challenged his thin and weakly looking *chi* (personal spirit) and was immediately killed. Since the Igbo world view was based on "discussion and consensus" (*Morning* 103) rather than on personal ambition and control, the anti-totalitarian slant of the story is a warning against seeking to control apparently weaker people. Achebe claims that even the Igbo deities are restricted in the power they have over earthly mortals, proving the innate love for freedom and possibility for dialogue with those higher up that Igbo traditions make available. Similarly, Achebe's fiction delivers the same warning. Both Okonkwo in *Things Fall Apart* (1958) and Ezeulu in *Arrow of God* (1964) fail in their respective attempts to remain in power, especially when they target their own people in their opposition to foreign invaders.

The checks and balances to prevent excessive power are imperative in neocolonial contexts which, according to Manning Marable in *African and Caribbean Politics*, have a general history of force and coercion employed in the process of colonialism. The past does indeed speak for the present since the "legacy of slavery, forced labor, and colonial rule" cannot be easily erased from the contemporary political scene in most African states (vii). The rash of one-party leadership and military regimes displays the continued concentration of power in the hands of a privileged few. According to Marable, the reliance on charismatic leaders to represent national liberation struggles in the past is partly responsible for leadership problems in the present. Charismatic figures who argued for mass struggle against colonialism at one point began to believe, after they had taken control of the government, that they had been responsible for the revolution. Marable mentions such leaders as Julius Nyerere of Tanzania, Leopold Senghor of Senegal, and Jomo Kenyatta of Kenya among a host of leaders who demanded independence from the colonial governments, but, on achieving their demands, reintroduced repressive measures against their critics and reproduced the humanitarian rhetoric of the colonizers to justify their authority. They claimed they knew what was good for the people, who became child-like mobs that needed to be disciplined in the interests of national solidarity and economic progress. The colonial practice of obliterating or dehumanizing the "natives" to excuse their exploitation was followed by the efforts of the petit-bourgeois leaders to silence the unidentified masses who had participated as much, if not more, in the struggle against colonialism.

The violent history of colonialism continues in contemporary Nigeria, as the conclusion of *A Man of the People* reveals. Economic power was often a corollary of political power, so party leaders would go to any lengths to win the election, using brute force where bribery could not achieve results. The complete breakdown of security as a result of the political thuggery of the leaders clears the stage for the deployment of military forces, resulting in an almost inevitable military takeover. The greed and unscrupulousness of the leaders who put their interests before those of their electorate ultimately result in cynicism on the part of the people and arrogance on the part of the military that now sets itself up as the messianic liberator of the country. But as Marable proves in his analysis of the US invasion of Grenada in 1983, any attempt to dictate theory from above to the supposedly ignorant masses will end in disaster (258). The alienation between the people and the leaders traps both in an endless circle of violence and repression.

Since independence in 1960, Nigeria has been under almost unbroken military rule. In the January 1966 coup, the armed forces had taken control in Nigeria ostensibly to control ethnic tensions and class conflicts, as various army leaders in different coups had asserted when they overthrew the preceding regime. Just as the colonial authorities had continued to deny independence, promising to give up power when the still immature natives were ready for it, military dictatorships often promise democracy when the indisciplined civilians are adequately controlled. In a state where ethnic tensions and class conflict along with illiteracy and diversity of the peasantry and working class diffuse the possibility of a coherent popular ideology, what Marable calls the "Bonapartist impulse" is given free rein (69). The coup attempt in Nigeria in April 1990 shows that religious tensions and clashes between the centre and the periphery have hardly been resolved. The rebellion against President General Ibrahim Babangida, who took control in a 1987 coup, was motivated by resentment against northern Muslim domination over the predominantly Christian and animist central and southern states. Significantly, the coup attempt began with plotters taking control of a radio station and broadcasting appeals for mass support. The recurring crises of coups and the huge demonstrations by students at Ibadan in support of the coup attempt (or at any rate the overthrow of the present regime) reveal the myth behind reports of a general contentment with military rule and the promise of stability that it ensures.

The move from a corrupt, inefficient neocolonial multiparty system to a rigid, authoritarian military state for whatever reason is hardly postcolonial progress, as far as Achebe is concerned. The regional and religious diversity is barely mentioned in *Anthills* since more space is given to the leadership that has failed to deal adequately with the pressures of nation building after independence. In the military dictatorships of Kangan in *Anthills*, the physical and ideological brutalization of the people continues under the leadership of Major John Ossai, Director of the State Research Police, a euphemism for the secret police. Sam's rise to unprecedented power is aided by the physical force of the police as "unconfirmed rumours of unrest,' secret trials, and executions in the barracks" seem to suggest (14).

The denial of mass participation in the interests of solidarity and stability is used as a glib excuse for continuing state power. Both Fanon and Marable emphasize the inclusion of the lower strata in social structures if a revolution is to succeed. Only the direct involvement of the masses can build the political and social consciousness necessary for the development of the nation. In *A Man of the People,* the intellectuals' attempt to mediate the stalemate between the corrupt and self-serving party leaders and the disillusioned and indifferent villagers fails to represent members of the lower classes, as Odili himself points out. The failure of the so-called "Common People's Convention" is ensured when Eunice announces that "the great revolutions of history were started by intellectuals, not the common people" (89). The reason the military regime takes control in a revolution that has the approval but not the direct participation of the people in the novel's conclusion is precisely because the lack of an organized mass revolt leaves the initiative for change with military coups or isolated attacks against individual leaders, as in the case of Eunice's assault on Chief Koko. In spite of the celebration in some quarters, Achebe does not lead us to believe that the military coup indicates an end to oppression, but, as in the case of leadership after independence, merely a change in the identity of the oppressors.

Achebe's focus in *Anthills* is not, as it first seems, on the three forces symbolized in the functions of Sam, Chris, and Ikem, or even Beatrice herself. He concentrates on the attempts to mute the voices of the people and on the struggle to tell the story. In a lecture at Sokoto in 1986, later published as "What Has Literature Got to Do With It?", Achebe valorizes the story as a preserver of heritage, custodian of tradition, and agent of change, three roles as we have seen, he demands of African writers. It prepares us, he claims, for the challenges of history. The dialectical relationship between the tale and the audience that demands that the tale be created as a strategy for survival is embodied in Achebe's continuum: "*People create stories create people;* or rather, *stories create people create stories*" (*Hopes and Impediments* 112).

Storytelling is therefore not merely a leisurely pursuit relegated to "creative writers" who are expected to perfect their art at the cost of its function, but an ongoing cultural process woven out of the fabric of daily living. The tales around the fireside in communal societies were told as much to transmit group identity and history as to provide guidelines to cope with the demands of one's environment. They sustained the tradition of resistance and grim survival that belong to the people rather than to any elite group. As Fanon says in *The Wretched of the Earth* of combative literature in the fighting phase of anti-colonialism:

> the storyteller replies to the expectant people by successive approximations, and makes his way, apparently alone but in fact helped on by his public, towards the seeking out of new patterns . . . the drama becomes . . . part of an action in preparation or already in progress (294).

The transformation of the story from an abstract act of communication intended for the pleasure of those who can "afford" (to understand) it to a concrete directive for popular action removes it from its elitist context of literary art and makes it available for mass consumption. Achebe clearly believes that writing and reading cannot be divorced from the larger context of political responsibility. The traditional function of the oral storyteller has not been discarded in *Anthills* even if it has changed slightly in an urban, literate context. While Beatrice acknowledges the contributions of "barely literate carpenters and artisans" who told political stories about animals and birds, the leader of the delegation from Abazon praises Ikem's editorial comments in his newspaper for the guidance they gave the villagers. The elder's own oratory convincingly presents the story of Abazon that has been dismissed without a hearing by the President. In the division of duties in preparing for the battle, actually fighting the battle, and surviving to tell the story of the struggle, the elder gives the story "the eagle feather" of ultimate achievement. With old age, he admits, he has come to realize that "only the story can continue beyond the war and the warrior" (124). Since even the storytellers are mortal, the story alone survives long after the fire is put out and the audience has retired for the day, its smouldering ashes a latent force readily available for future appropriation and renewal of the battle.

One instance of the story's endless capacities to meet the changing needs of the audience is Ikem's lecture to the student community, "The Tortoise and the Leopard—a political meditation on the importance of struggle," an adaptation of the elder's anecdote. Neither the old man's imprisonment nor Ikem's suspension detract from the effect the account has on the audience. On the contrary, both the official acts of silencing only serve to make Ikem's narrative even more explosive in its defiance. The lively participation of the audience is sufficiently threatening to the state authorities who react by murdering Ikem. But as the old man believes, regardless of the transience of the artist and the audience and even the historical moment that engendered the story, the tale will survive. Long after the deaths of important figures in Kangan, the germ of social transformation continues to be "alive and kicking" like Elewa's newborn. As Emmanuel, the President of the Students' Union admits, "It wasn't Ikem the Man who changed me. I hardly knew him. It was his ideas set on paper" (223). The naming ceremony that concludes the novel is less a tribute to Ikem, the child's father, and Chris, than a grim recognition of the fact that the struggle must continue in the wake of yet another coup. Indeed, the casual dismissal of leadership by the ragged peasants celebrating the disappearance of His Excellency signifies that "soja come, soja gwo" but the people, like the story, will endure (222).

The novel is not, as Chris's dying words prove, about the "three green bottles" who are swiftly eliminated and whose loss is felt by only a few individuals. It is the story of the people who survive yet another crisis with their usual resilience. Achebe does not sentimentalize the masses here any more than he does in the more cynical *A Man of the People.* In a general condition of military rule, armed robberies, and public executions, the dehumanization of the people and their tolerance of corrupt leadership is subject to critique, which, as we see in Ikem's fiery lecture, Achebe does not neglect. But this does not call for a complete dismissal of the people's revolutionary potential and their ability to resist the leaders who, in the luxury of their private retreats, have forgotten them. The problem lies, as Ikem realizes, not in the failure of the masses, but in the failure of those in power "to re-establish vital inner links with the poor and dispossessed of this country" (141).

The "return of utterance" to Beatrice is a triumph of the people's struggle, in spite of failed leadership and betrayed hopes (220). Her flat becomes the space for class and gender affiliations that express opposition to the current power structure. Beatrice's own separation from the marketwomen and taxi-drivers and her superior attitude to her maid Agatha are reworked through the crisis in her life caused by the deaths of both Chris and Ikem. Her isolated home becomes the refuge of Emmanuel the student leader, Braimoh the taxi driver, and Adamma, the nurse. This breakdown of class and gender barriers and the potential for such an alliance is underlined by the naming ritual usually performed by men but which is now taken over by the women. Elewa's child is given a boy's name, Amaechina, "may-the-path-never-close" (222). Amaechina's birth in a period of social unrest through a union between a middle-class male intellectual and an illiterate working class woman suggests the emergent bonding between classes and the unlimited possibilities that such a "path" opens up. The toast at the end of the ritual is to "People and Ideas."

Achebe's renewed faith in the "stubborn sense of community" articulates and establishes the dialogic relationship between the story, the writer, and the audience. Literature is the discursive field in which these three elements engage in a political exchange that mediates aresponse to current social issues. The writer's task is not necessarily to lead the people in their confrontation with unjust power structures, but to point out the legitimacy of their cause and their capacity to triumph. The story functions as one aspect of their political education, providing them with the necessary information and direction to empower themselves. As Fanon points out in *The Wretched of the Earth:*

> What [political education] means is to try, relentlessly and passionately, to teach the masses that everything depends on them . . . that there is no such thing as a demiurge . . . but that the demiurge is the people themselves and the magic hands are finally only the hands of the people (157-58).

One of the problems with using literature as a means of political education, however, is that "the people" in most postcolonial countries are still mostly illiterate and very often do not know English, the language many African writers choose as their medium. Ngugi addressed this problem by writing in Gikuyu: his first novel in Gikuyu, *Caitaani Mutharaba-ini,* was read aloud in rural areas to those who could not read. Achebe, on the other hand, continues to use English since he feels that it is the most viable means of communication in a country with many different languages and ethnic groups. While his works are read by a predominantly educated, middle-class audience, it is still important to remember his inclusion of the lower-classes. What is even more important is the contribution the masses make to the political education of writers and intellectuals. The elder from Abazon, for instance, radicalizes Ikem's politics and forces him to rethink his own attitude towards the peasants. The need "to *re-form*" the story to provide space to those voices that have been muted gives relevance to Ikem's "ideas," making them concrete realities that pave the way for social change. In Achebe's view, the task of the writer extends beyond recording the past accurately to actually influencing the course of events in the future. Indeed, social participation is almost inevitable. The demands of history transform Chris and Ikem from "witnesses" into participants.

In a discussion at the University of Massachussets in 1988, Achebe maintains that the writer's participation in his social milieu must be defined by the inevitable conflict between art and authority (Chametzky 74). As he puts it, both the emperor and the poet should pay attention to each other. So forcefully disturbing must the writer be in his challenge to the emperor's power, that the emperor has "to sit up and ask Where is that man? Go and get him" (74). In this radical perspective of the writer's role in society, not until the author's very life is at stake is the story completely and successfully told.

Anthills of the Savannah: Postmodern or Postcolonial Novel?

VINEY KIRPAL

Until the publication of *Anthills of the Savannah,* the reception of Achebe's novels in the West had been a mixed one. For example, *Things Fall Apart* (1958) was a hit in England more for its exotic quality than its other virtues. In America, its reception was lukewarm (Eko). There was greater interest in *No Longer at Ease* (1960) because of its individualized portraits, but not in England where readers were looking for a second exotic novel. *Arrow of God* (1964) was, for the same reason, received well in England but not in America. *A Man of the People* (1966) was liked in England because the English were familiar with that kind of Nigeria, while in America the enthusiasm for Achebe's works reportedly rose with this novel (Eko). However, it is *Anthills of the Savannah* (1987), his latest novel, that has had a resounding reception not only in England and America but also in Sweden and the other Scandinavian countries (Granqvist). The overwhelming success in the West can be related to its supposedly postmodern literary qualities and its overtly feminist stance. Ironically, this novel, which is more relevant to Nigeria than to any other country, was earlier not received well on home territory (Granqvist). Equally ironic is the fact that its evaluation as a postmodern feminist novel (a consequence of Euro-American readings) has now begun to affect even Nigerian critics in their re-readings of the novel. At the international symposium for Chinua Achebe's sixtieth birthday held at the University of Nigeria, Nsukka, in February 1990, a

Nigerian critic dramatically declared that "storytelling" and "teaching" were clichés that Achebe in this novel had to leave behind in order to get on with postmodernism in his journey towards artistic maturity (Yerima).

In this essay I wish to oppose the view that *Anthills* is a postmodern novel by demonstrating that the techniques used (as in all his fiction) have their origin in the Nigerian oral narrative tradition. Similarly, its explicitly political theme, as in his other novels, is rooted in postcolonial compulsions. Again, in keeping with the Nigerian reality *Anthills* is a womanist (not a feminist) novel. It posits freedom for women through reformation and not through revolution. The novel is not an avant-garde, aesthetic genre (Wilson). It neither indulges in intellectual titillation of formal experiments in fragmentation (Tiffin) nor in foregrounding the textual gaps produced by the system of writing itself (Hutcheon quoting Slemon 151). Unlike postmodern novels, it is not politically ambivalent (Hutcheon) and it does not depict an individual existentialist impasse through black humour and "jouissance of contemporary post-structuralist theories of 'powerful' play" (Griffiths 133). In place of linguistic games (Bell 245), the novel addresses itself to problems relevant to Nigerian society. Like most postcolonial novels, *Anthills* aims at social change instituted within the Nigerian "core of reality." It is an optimistic work—despite the death of three major characters—in which the surviving characters try to transcend present restrictions by imagining and attempting to create a better future Nigerian society.

Two pivotal chapters of *Anthills* are devoted to establishing the importance, not of writing, but of storytelling. In chapter nine, titled "Views of Struggle," the old man of Abazon celebrates the act of storytelling as more significant than war or history:

> It is the story, not the others [war-drums and the exploits of brave fighters], that saves our progeny from blundering like blind beggars. . . . [The] story

> is everlasting. . . . Like fire, when it is not blazing it is smouldering under its own ashes or sleeping and resting inside its flint-house (124).

Storytelling takes primacy over other activities, because it subverts the lies of history and opposes political authoritarianism. That is why not everybody can become a storyteller. It is the boon that Agwu (the god of healers) grants to the chosen one:

> Agwu picks his disciple, rings his eye with white chalk and dips his tongue, willing or not, in the brew of prophecy; and right away the man will speak and put head and tail back to the severed trunk of our tale (125).

Storytellers are special people because they tell of unrecorded, unmarked tales of struggle against oppression. In exemplification, the old man narrates the story of the tortoise and the leopard and likens the struggle of the people of Abazon against the military regime of Kangan to the "struggle" between the puny tortoise and the strong leopard. Although unevenly matched, the tortoise had swung into action on the road, scratching wildly with his hands and feet and throwing sand in all directions. When the puzzled leopard had wanted to know why the tortoise had done that, the tortoise had replied:

> *Because even after I am dead I would want anyone passing by this spot to say, yes, a fellow and his match struggled here* (128; emphasis in original).

The old man concludes that the people of Abazon were fighting a powerful regime "perhaps to no purpose except with the hope that those who come after us will be able to say '*True, our fathers were defeated but they tried*'" (128; italics in original). The moral of the story is that it is imperative to struggle when governments become repressive and tyrannical. The old man's spirited narration highlights through suggestion the moral failure on the part of the political elite of Bassa (men like Chris, Okong) who were quietly acquiescing in the authoritarianism of the present regime.

For speaking out against military dictators, the old man is arrested shortly after and held in solitary confinement in Bassa Maximum Security Prison (BMSP). In chapter twelve, Ikem narrates to Bassa university students the same story of the tortoise and the leopard and observes that storytellers always run a great risk because they challenge power groups—political, religious, academic:

> [S]torytellers are a threat. They threaten all champions of control, they frighten usurpers of the right-to-freedom of the human spirit—in state, in church or mosque, in party congress, in the university or wherever. . . (153).

Ikem, like the old man, is arrested soon after and killed in a fake encounter with the security officers.

In *Anthills*, Achebe fictionalizes the condition of the activist artist in Nigeria under a repressionist regime. Subtly, he re-establishes the connection between the role of the traditional artist (who had subverted the power of the colonial regime with his stories) and the contemporary writer who challenges his own leaders. Wole Soyinka, Christopher Okigbo (Ikem's original), Achebe—all suffered during the civil war but like the traditional storyteller, they did not give up recording the story of their struggles against tyrannical regimes. In this novel, Achebe reaffirms the role of the novelist as teacher spelt out at the time of writing *Things Fall Apart* (*Morning* 42-45).

In a recent interview, Argentinian-born writer Andrew Graham-Yooll, the newly-appointed editor of *Index on Censorship*, was asked which writers, in his opinion, had contributed most to the cause of freedom of expression and human rights. Graham-Yooll replied:

> That is a wide-ranging question. In Latin America, you could include any writer of any status. Writers there have a political responsibility as soon as they rise above the rest. They are contributors to thought, to debate, to discussion. The writer—this is rather oriental—the writer, because he can read and convey an impression in a beautiful language, becomes a natural representative of those who cannot speak for themselves. Amado of Brazil says: 'the writer is trusted, the politicians are not.' So the writer becomes a politician (3-5).

Achebe in *Anthills* is saying nearly the same thing. Except that for "writer" he substitutes "storyteller." According to him, the storyteller is a gifted person who with imagination and fervour speaks on behalf of those who cannot. That is why the storyteller is trusted, while politicians (and their tailored histories) are not. Therefore, storytellers are activists. Achebe has always seen Nigerian "writers" as the direct descendants of storytellers rather than of literate writers in the Western sense. The traditional storyteller was a person who was not concerned merely with the aesthetic aspects of art and entertainment but also with values and socio-political change. Art in Nigeria was never an autotelic activity as it has been for the artist in the West. Therefore, instead of formalistic experiments and intellectual language games, it is a fictional blueprint for political and social regeneration that Achebe has given us in *Anthills*.

Interestingly in both chapters nine and twelve the old man and Ikem (while speaking on the primariness of storytellers and storytelling) draw upon the traditional skills of oratory. The art of oratory in West Africa, particularly among the Igbos, is known to have been carried to remarkable perfection (Finnegan 444). Achebe has observed of the Igbo that "the finest examples of prose occur not in those forms [folktales, legends, proverbs and riddles] but in oratory and even in the art of good conversation" (Quoted in Finnegan 445). Ruth Finnegan has related the phenomenon to the absence of the written word for formalized transactions and artistic expressions, and the concomitant development of the oral skill of public speaking to perform these functions (445). Oratory therefore falls between highly conventional literary expression and informal everyday conversation (445). Often proverbs are used in oratory to appeal to the audience or to make a point with extra forcefulness. In *Anthills*, the old man of Abazon typically chooses his allusions and proverbs with consummate skill:

> *. . . [The] cock that crows in the morning belongs to one household but his voice is the property of the neighbourhood. You should be proud that this bright cockerel [Ikem] that wakes the whole village [Kangan/ Nigeria] comes from your compound.*
>
> There was such compelling power and magic in his voice that even the MC who had voiced the complaints was now beginning to nod his head, like everybody else, in agreement (122; emphasis added).

The technique employed both in the old man's speech and in Ikem's lecture (he calls it a meditation) is therefore the method of skilled traditional orators: they made sure of audience participation in a way analogous to storytelling. For example, they expected murmurs of support and agreement, muttered rejoinders to their rhetorical questions, laughter when they purposely brought in something amusing or exaggerated. Consider, for instance, how both the old man and Ikem essay to get the desired response:

> (i) So fully is [the storyteller] owned by the telling sometimes . . . he will turn the marks left on him by the chickenpox and yaws he suffered in childhood into bullet scars. . . .
>
> *The tense air was broken suddenly by loud laughter. The old man himself smiled with be-*

> *nign mischief* (125; emphasis in original).

> (ii) 'There has been, for a few years now, a running battle between me and the Civil Service Union. You know that, don't you?' *Yes*, roared the audience, laughing. . . . 'Those of you who follow our battles may remember that it all came to a head last year when I wrote a stinging editorial on the eve of their Annual Congress.' There was smiling recognition on some faces, some nodding of the head and scattered remnants of laughter (157).

In this context, it may be observed that *Anthills* is not the only novel where Achebe has employed the traditional skills of oratory. In *Arrow of God,* which has several excellent public debates, the one between Ezeulu and Nwaka (on whether or not to go to war with Okperi) is memorable for its dramatic quality and impact (16). Similarly, in *Things Fall Apart,* the oldest member of the *ummuna* uses oratorical skills in his farewell speech to Okonkwo (150). Obi Okonkwo's maiden speech to the Umuofia Progressive Union in *No Longer at Ease* has been prepared according to familiar Igbo oratorical practices, and as intended, draws the approval of the audience who nod their heads and make suitable rejoinders (81).

In *Anthills*, Achebe has not only used the traditional oratorical skills but as in his earlier novels has also made subtle use of yet another oral narrative form—that of the prayer. According to Finnegan, the prayer is a type of formal speech without being as lengthy and elaborate as formal oratory but with a tendency to become stylized (456). The important feature of a prayer is that it can have both a conventionally recognized overall form—a "literary" genre as it were—and also provide scope for individual variation according to speaker and context (457). In chapter eighteen of the novel, a prayer is extemporized by Elewa's uncle to bless Elewa's newborn baby girl. While, as is conventional, the prayer makes striking use of repetition in the form of parallelisms through which the power of God is progressively described and the newborn welcomed, Elewa's uncle also extemporizes and adds new ideas and requests of his own:

> 'Owner of the world: Man of countless names! The church people call you three-in-one. It is a good name. But it carries miserly and insufficient praise. Four-hundred-in-one would seem more fitting in our eyes. . . .'
>
> 'What brings us here is the child you sent us. May her path be straight. . . .'
>
> '*Ise*!' replied all the company.
>
> 'May she have life and may her mother have life.'
>
> '*Ise*!'
>
> 'What happened to her father, may it not happen again.'
>
> '*Ise*!'
>
> 'When I asked who named her they told me All of Us. May this child be the daughter of all of us.'
>
> '*Ise!*.'
>
> 'May all of us have life!'
>
> '*Ise*!'
>
> 'May these young people here when they make the plans for their world not forget her. And all other children.'
>
> '*Ise*!'
>
> 'May they also remember useless old people like myself and Elewa's mother when they are making their plans.'
>
> '*Ise*!' (227-228).

In *Anthills*, where the controlling motif is struggle against authoritarian regimes, the selfishness of the educated elite and its compliance with those in power is its ancillary theme. Sam the dictator, Chris the Minister for Information. Ikem the editor of the *National Gazette* and Beatrice the Senior Assistant Secretary in the Ministry of Finance are London University products who are equally indicted. These intellectuals, each bright in his/her own way and very well-placed, are completely alienated from the people and insular in their privileges. With the exception (to some extent) of Ikem, they love the trappings of power, are weak and bourgeois in their mentality (though they do change in the end as a result of their experiences). An analysis of a few telling incidents from the novel will bear this out.

This novel opens with His Excellency, Sam, chairing a Cabinet meeting. Instead of transacting serious business, he behaves like a power-drunk, insecure military dictator bullying eleven intelligent men (including Chris) who willingly play the buffoon and fan his vanity. As they sit in the hermetically sealed room, a great noise breaks in from the window in the east:

> "A storm?" someone asks.
>
> The low hibiscus hedge outside the window and its many brilliant red bells stood still and unruffled. . . . It was no ordinary storm.
>
> The Chief Secretary whose presence of mind is only inhibited by the presence of His Excellency moves over to the sill, unhooks a latch and pushes back a glass window. *And the world surges into the alien climate of the Council Chamber* on a violent wave of heat and *the sounds of a chanting multitude.* And His Excellency rushes back into the room at the same time leaving the huge doors swinging.
>
> 'What is going on?' he demands frantically (9; emphases added).

The passage highlights the unusual fear and terrible insecurity in which all authoritarian leaders (particularly military dictators) live. The chants of the peaceful six-member delegation from Abazon (supported by indigenes in Bassa) get mistaken for the storm of revolution about to break upon the impregnable Presidential Palace. Through the use of the colonizer's expression "multitudes" (for people) the novelist draws attention to the enormous distance between the rulers and the ruled. Sam and his ministers, he suggests, have merely stepped into the shoes of the white masters. Their alienation from those they are supposed to serve is captured in the phrases "alien climate of the Council Chamber," and "violent wave of heat" that contrasts the conditions of drought in the country with the luxury of air-conditioners inside the Council Chamber.

Despite his proclaimed concern for the poor, Ikem is no different. In her study, Lyn Innes has pointed out the gap between Ikem's pious pronouncements on the dispossessed and the poor of Nigeria and his actual feelings for them. She cites the episode of the traffic jam (and Ikem's effort not to let the two taxi-drivers overtake him), and the incident where he insensitively packs off Elewa to her home at midnight because he can't bear to keep a lower-class woman in his house through the night. Although Ikem is ideologically involved in the lives of the down and out and he overtly crusades their cause, it is as true that in a few specific cases his treatment of them, initially at least, leaves much to be desired. For example, though the old man calls him a brilliant son of Abazon, it is a fact that Ikem has never visited his village even once since his departure from it in youth. Similarly, his inconsiderate behaviour towards Elewa is contrasted in the novel with his sensitivity and correct behaviour towards Beatrice, an economic, intellectual equal. In her memoirs, Beatrice tells of the incident in London when she had been abandoned at a dance by her Nigerian boyfriend in favour of a white girl. Alone and humiliated, she had left the hall and called up Ikem who had immediately undertaken a hazardous journey on tubes and buses from South London well after midnight to reach her home at half-past three, his lips too frozen to speak (92).

Ikem undergoes a great change, however, after his meeting with the old man of Abazon, and the visit to his home by the two taxi-drivers whom he had bullied in the traffic jam. While the old man had urged him to repeat the story of the struggle of the Abazonians against the powerful rulers of Kangan/Nigeria, the taxi-drivers had come to thank him for his commitment (as editor of *National Gazette*) to their upliftment. Their visit particularly exhilarates him because it signifies reaffirmation of his social goals. For the first time he is able to articulate his real problem to himself:

> [H]e had always had the necessity in a vague but insistent way, had always felt a yearning without very clear definition, to connect his essence with earth and earth's people. The problem for him had never been whether it should be done but how to do it with integrity (140-41).

The night of the taxi-drivers' visit becomes a night of fulfillment for him, and he and Elewa make love as they never had before. Their union symbolizes the total and true fusion of the intellectual with the earth and earth's people. Significantly, the child that is conceived that night and born posthumously is named Amaechina. Amaechina means "May-the-path-never-close" (222) and suggests the utopian vision of oneness between Nigeria's elite and her people.

Beatrice's initial distance from the common people is similarly conveyed in her arrogant relationship with Agatha, her housemaid. Theirs is a replay of the master-slave relationship of colonial times. Two women living under the same roof, mutually dependent on each other—one for her job, the other for her housekeeping—theirs is an uneasy relationship. The blame is clearly placed at Beatrice's door by the author who suggests that those who are in a dominant position must reach out to those subordinate. Instead of kindness, Beatrice displays rudeness and meanness towards Agatha who retaliates by showing a "slave's" sullen disobedience—defiance, sulking or tears. It is only after the death of Ikem and after she has taken Elewa into her flat following Elewa's threatened miscarriage that it dawns on her that were she only more sympathetic towards Agatha, probably the latter too would behave differently. One day, after Beatrice has rebuked Agatha sharply over her misconduct to Elewa ("Agatha, you are a very stupid girl and a very wicked girl. . . . Get out of my way!" 182), she sees her sitting bunched up in the kitchen, her face buried in her hands, crying. Suddenly she feels sorry for the girl and placing her hand on her shoulder, she apologizes:

> 'I am sorry Agatha.'
>
> The unbelief [of Agatha] turned first to shock and then, through the mist of her tears, a sunrise of smiles (185).

The incident is important because for the first time Beatrice consciously attempts to establish contact with a common person (her relationship with Elewa is more an outgrowth of her feelings for Ikem and therefore not a consciously chosen relationship). Earlier she would sometimes bar Agatha geographically by locking her out of the main house or by confining her to the kitchen (110). Now, by placing her hand on Agatha's shoulder, she literally and symbolically makes the same contact that Ikem (the intellectual) had made with Elewa (the earth's people).

Chris's relationship with the common people is never clearly defined. He does have a houseboy whom he probably treats well. Agatha also likes him. However, Chris is a member of the Cabinet and therefore possibly as alienated from the people as any other member. A change comes into his life when, disguised as a poor motor mechanic, he is forced to flee Bassa in the company of Emmanuel the student-leader and Braimoh the taxi-driver who shelters him from the police for some days in his house. By wearing a common worker's clothes, Chris symbolically identifies with the poor. Two significant realizations come to him on his journey to Abazon. The first is that although bright, talented people exist among the lower classes, the elite always believe that they alone are important to the running of a country (He calls Sam, Ikem and himself the three green bottles that hang precariously from the wall looking down pompously upon the world unaware that they can fall down any time). The other realization comes to him when dressed as a mechanic but unable to behave like one, he is nearly discovered by the soldier on duty. His remark, "To succeed as small man no be small thing" (194), conveys the difficulty of the power groups in even imaginarily reducing the distance between themselves and the people of the earth. Significantly, as the novel ends, we are told that "Chris, in spite of his brilliance, was just beginning to be vaguely aware of people like that old man [Elewa's uncle]" (232).

Interestingly, as each of the central characters (with the exception of Sam who is killed in a coup) matures in his/her relationship with the people, the language of the novel formally enacts the erasure of colonial attitudes and values. The first two chapters are presented in standard English with proverbs being used by Professor Okong, a member of the Cabinet, to evoke a tribal identity; Sam, who dislikes the use of proverbs, says, "I don't quite get you, Professor. Please cut out the proverbs, if you don't mind" (19), signaling that he sees himself as a Westernized, secular person. In this section, the author is critical of both types—the people affecting tribal discourse and those who are Westernized. In the later chapters, particularly in chapter eighteen of the novel, not only proverbs but pidgin too is used by all the characters—Chris, Beatrice, Emmanuel, Captain Abdul Medani, Braimoh, Agatha, Aina, Elewa, Elewa's mother and her uncle. The use of proverbs and pidgin as normal discourse characterizes decolonization and a repudiation of the artificial distance set up by the colonizer between ruler and ruled. The method is exactly the reverse of the method in *Things Fall Apart* where the novel is replete with proverbs in parts I and II while part III is in standard English and pidgin. In *Things Fall Apart*, pidgin is spoken by the intermediary class of court messengers suggesting a colonized mentality. But in *Anthills* pidgin has become the legitimate language of the common people while standard English represents the language of the elite of Nigeria.

In the novel, the legend of Idemili is told in detail to reaffirm the intricate Igbo philosophy about rulers. In traditional Africa, power was completely decentralized and not concentrated in the hands of one individual, be he the king or a tribal chief or the chief priest. The punishment for overreaching was always severe, and the Igbo attitude to power was built into its folklore. In *Arrow of God,* Achebe had depicted the consequences of Ezeulu's defiant transgression of the limits of his power. In *Anthills*, the same belief is conveyed through the rise and fall of Sam as dictator metaphorized in the story of the man who dared to challenge Idemili's authority (104-5). According to the legend, the Almighty sent his own daughter, Idemili, to earth to ensure that moral law, peace and modesty would clothe authority (102). The legend warns against the sad end of the one who, in defiance of Idemili, possesses an "unquenchable thirst to sit in authority on his fellows" (104). Sam was not a bad man to begin with, we are told. It was only after being installed as dictator that he gradually developed an "unquenchable thirst" for power, renouncing old friendships, sacking dissidents and fostering sycophancy. The one courageous effort that Beatrice, an old friend, makes to bring him back to the path of righteousness, is haughtily spurned by him (81). Not only is Beatrice not recognized by him as the Priestess of Idemili (the other persona that she is given in the novel) trying to give him one more chance, she is also disgraced and humiliated and turned out of his party. Sam's tryst with the Priestess marks the beginning of the end for him. The episode is only a contemporary version of the ancient legend, the details have changed but the core meaning remains. Like the impudent man in the traditional legend, Sam is punished with death.

In the novel, we are also told that Sam would never have become as powerful as he did but for the silence of the self-seeking men (including Chris) around him. Chris is as much responsible for Sam's unchecked growth to authority as the others in the Cabinet. In the very opening chapter, we see him explaining his silence as "detached clinical interest" (2). Like Odili in *A Man of the People*, Chris has adopted the policy of appeasement toward Sam and the tragedy is that he feels no guilt over his own moral deterioration:

> 'I am sorry, Your Excellency. But I have no difficulty swallowing *and* digesting your rulings.' . . . But he was not appeased. . . . Without raising my eyes I said again: 'I am very sorry, Your Excellency.' A year ago I would never have said it again that second time—*without doing grave violence to myself.* Now I did it *like a casual favour* to him. It *meant nothing at all to me—no inconvenience whatever*—and yet everything to him (1, emphases added).

He rationalizes his lack of integrity by saying that he has despaired of fighting the dictator, and has no energy left to resign from the Cabinet or to go into political exile (118). His so-called "reasonableness," "considerateness," and discretion are clearly ploys adopted to enable him to stay on in power. His advice to Beatrice to "stay cool" at Sam's party (she had been invited there without Chris) no matter what the provocation and to "keep all options open" (73) does not speak highly of the man who is going to marry her. In some ways, his lack of understanding of Beatrice's state of mind over the humiliating episode at Sam's party is akin to Ikem's insensitivity towards Elewa in packing her off to her home in the middle of the night.

That brings one to the question: Is *Anthills* a feminist novel? Although Beatrice describes Chris as "entirely different" from other men and as very understanding (about her) even "without asking a single question," (89) the events in the novel (for example, her misunderstanding with him, 111-13) do not seem to bear it out. The resolution of their misunderstanding in passionate love-making (113-14) seems only like a romantic twist given to a very serious issue—namely, integrity in any relationship—which remains unconfronted by the novelist. If to sleep with a man is the definition of feminism, then it is a rather limited one.

Both Chris and Ikem respect and feel awed by Beatrice and Elewa more for their goddesslike stance (114) than for their qualities as distinct human beings. The fact that they believe the two girls to be worthy of worship only as Mother/Priestess/ Goddess (Beatrice is likened to Mother Idoto and Elewa to the godlike spirit of the masked maiden 175, 184) implies that they are tradition-bound men. Ikem professes to have tremendous respect for market women, peasant women and intellectual women, but his initial behaviour with Elewa does not support his claim, though it is true towards Beatrice. Chris declares Beatrice to be his ideal woman (66-67) but he is extra-careful not to upset her only in her "goddessy," statesque posture; else, she is no more than a sex object (115, 199).

What about the women? Beatrice is portrayed as a young urban professional who places her career before marriage, has an independent establishment, makes careful relationships with men and has chosen her own future husband. Elewa is a half-literate, poor girl who is the daughter of an ordinary market woman. She is very attractive, works as a salesgirl in a perfume shop and is the kind who, after a lovers' tiff, will take the first step to make up with her man. Between Beatrice and Elewa, who is the more liberated? On the surface of it, it seems it is Beatrice. But what is the reality? Beatrice is assertive only in her divine statesque posture, but otherwise she is quite vulnerable to Chris's charms. For example, she takes him to task for not caring sufficiently about what happened to her at the party at Abichi (113) but easily dissolves into tears and melts on an embrace and a kiss from Chris. Her ideological conflict forgotten, she yields totally to him and even serves him food she cooks herself (116). Elewa, similarly, forgives Ikem (without his apologizing for having sent her away from his flat at midnight) and calls him up at his office the following day asking him to take her to the beach in the afternoon to buy fresh fish from the fishermen coming ashore so that "I go cook you nice pepper soup, today" (36). Both girls, therefore, irrespective of the difference in class and education, share patriarchal values. Neither is liberated. By contrast, consider Ekwefi, the second wife of Okonkwo in *Things Fall Apart.* Ekwefi had left her husband to come to live with Okonkwo and marry him. Despite the traditional manner in which Achebe has painted her portrait, Ekwefi emerges as a highly individualistic, spirited character. She does not fear Okonkwo and she never makes an effort to placate or humour him. Though Okonkwo, a traditional husband, beats her sometimes, there is no doubt about his deep love and care for Ekwefi. This is most evident in the scene in which Chielo the Priestess carries off their daughter Ezinma to the Cave of the Oracle (98-99). Neither Beatrice nor Elewa has Ekwefi's spirit of independence and freedom. Even Clara in *No Longer at Ease* is more assertive than these two girls. Although pregnant, she chooses to get an abortion and repudiate Obi when she realizes he is not strong enough to stand by her (145). In *Anthills*, on the other hand, the men take advantage of their women, and the women, after a small fuss, rush to placate them.

A critic (Lyn Innes) wonders why the relationships of Chris and Ikem with their women are left unresolved in the novel. The point can be explained by comparing *Anthills* with a thematically similar West Indian novel, *Natives of My Person* by George Lamming. In *Natives of My Person*, the new leaders are shown to be power-hungry men, happy to be within the magic circle of power and to oppress their womenfolk. Pinteados, the Spanish pilot of their ship remarks on their exploitative, irresponsible relationships with their women:

> '. . . To feel authority over the women! That was enough for them. But to commit themselves fully to what they felt authority over. That they could never master. Such power they were afraid of' (325).

Anthills is a novel about power (of rulers, men) versus powerlessness (of the people, women). That is where the themes of political and gender inequality coalesce in the novel. There is a suggestion that, in both power and gender politics, the dominant groups must learn to bridge the distance with the subordinate group and respect the latter's dignity. Again, the novel is a womanist novel (suggesting reformation of the lives of women) and not a feminist (militant, revolutionary) novel. In a lengthy discussion between Ikem and Beatrice in chapter seven, the difference between reformation and revolution is pointed out. Revolution, explains Ikem, may be a necessary phase in the liberation of any society but "it does not confer freedom" on it in the long run (99). Reform, by contrast, "may be a dirty word then but it begins to look more and more like the most promising route to success in the real world" (99). If a society is to be changed, it must not be disturbed at its core because that would invite disaster. A society must therefore only be re-formed "around what it is, its core of reality; not around an intellectual abstraction" (100).

Similarly, the liberation of women in Nigeria can best be achieved not through revolution (violence, militancy, feminism) but through re-formation (Achebe goes to the original meaning of the word) built around the core of reality in that society. Neither Elewa's way (passive, traditional) nor Beatrice's (active, Western) will help women's liberation. A new role for woman has to be found without doing violence to the essentially Nigerian values. A sample of the new role for the Nigerian woman is provided (in fictional terms) in chapter eighteen of the novel.

Achebe is as critical of Westernization (a form of colonization) in this novel as in his other novels. One telling incident shows how he regards alienation from indigenous traditions, and acculturation to the white man's ways. The incident concerns the management of grief in Nigerian and Western societies respectively. In this episode Elewa becomes the symbol of the traditional value system. On hearing of the suspension of Ikem as editor, Elewa uninhibitedly bursts into tears and cries violently (149). The authorial voice intervenes to observe: "All three

[Beatrice, Chris and Ikem] were embarrassed by this intrusive emotion. . ." (149). They are embarrassed by Elewa's "undignified" display of emotion, because it is the way of a "backward" culture. By contrast, Beatrice (in true British tradition) suppresses her grief after Chris's death, sometimes going to the privacy of her bedroom to weep but never weeping in the presence of her friends. In their presence she always tries to present a calm and composed countenance:

> Beatrice rushed away into her bedroom.
>
> Elewa followed after her. . . . After a few minutes Elewa came back.
>
> 'Is she all right?' asked Abdul a little ahead of other inquirers.
>
> 'No trouble. To cry small no be bad thing,' . . .
>
> 'Madam too strong,' said Agatha. 'To strong too much no de good for woman.'
>
> 'E no good for anybody whether na man-o or na woman-o, na the same thing,' said Elewa. . . (230).

Elewa recovers from her grief much quicker than Beatrice from hers because instead of expressing it freely (the Nigerian way), the latter tends to bottle it up (the English way). The above-quoted conversation shows the absence of a higher valorization on masculine toughness for both men and women in the traditional Nigerian concept of life epitomized in the worldview of the uneducated people of Nigeria—people like Elewa and Agatha who were never exposed to Westernization as the educated people are.

The implication of this scene for the woman question is immense. Woman's liberation lies not in attempting to become like a man—for example by placing her career before marriage, being aggressively ambitious, taking the initiative in lovemaking—but by freeing herself from patriarchal values and psychological subordination to men. This would mean that the

Nigerian woman's growth and freedom should not occur in the Western feminist way but in a way that is in consonance with the "core of reality" of her own society. The men too, by realizing both masculine and feminine qualities (a concept intrinsic to Igbo society and expressed powerfully in *Things Fall Apart*) would be able to remove their domination (originating in brute physical strength) over the women.

In a novel which is about the oppressed of the world—the common people, women—it is significant to note that it begins with the voice of a powerful dictator and a male, and concludes with the voice of Elewa, a common person and a woman. The shift in values, necessary for the Nigeria of the future, is thus adroitly conveyed. The world shall belong to woman because it is only when Idemili's daughter is in supremacy that power is checked by peace, modesty and moral law. The world shall belong to "the people of the world" because it was always theirs. Just as when everything is destroyed in brush fires that consume the country's savannahs, the ants waiting in the womb of the *Anthills* come out and show their solidarity, so do the people of the world who survive the fires of tyrannical history come out and tell the truth through their stories.[1] Achebe joins hands with the common people/storytellers to tell the story of Nigeria, of her political brush fires and of her women. He does it not like an apolitical postmodernnist but like the solicitous postcolonial he has always been.

NOTE

1. This was the explanation of the title of the novel offered by some Nigerian critics during the discussion of *Anthills of the Savannah* at the Symposium for Chinua Achebe's Sixtieth Birthday held at the University of Nigeria, Nsukka, Nigeria, Feb, 12-14, 1990.

Anthills of the Savannah and the Poetics of Despair and Hope

ASHLEY HALPÉ

At the time of writing the guns have started up again in the North and the East. When I was at the corner shop of a Colombo suburb last night, two ambulances screamed past. The drivers were in uniform. They were rushing wounded airlifted from the North to the military hospital. . . .

I begin again. When I wrote my proposal for this paper I found it possible to say:

> Reading *Anthills* in today's Lanka is an unnerving experience. One would imagine that we have made news enough, that we have plumbed depths. But *Anthills* offers chilling reminders and prophecies of a worse that might yet be. We haven't yet experienced open dictatorships, public executions. . . .

And we hadn't yet experienced anything like the killing of Ikem Osodi. Not two weeks later:

> In the early hours of Sunday (18 Feb) a group of armed men who arrived in a Pajero jeep [sic] dragged out Richard de Zoysa and ordered him to board the jeep [sic]. That was the last time his mother and three other occupants of his Nawala residence saw him alive. His body was washed ashore at Koralawella, a fishing village about two miles away from Mora-

> tuwa, on the southern highway.
> Richard was the first so-called 'anti-establishment' journalist to get killed at the hands of death squad men better known as 'vigilantes.' . . (Ferdinando).

The aim of this somewhat unorthodox opening is to suggest that certain times and places can impart deeper resonances, sharper relevances, to the poetics of an *Anthills*. Correspondingly, although the novel was widely acclaimed and made the shortlist for the 1987 Booker Prize, not a few of the responses seem more than a little off-centre, at times bizarre:

> This is a poet's novel without being a poetic one . . (Brownjohn 59).

> There is a world in these individuals. Chinua Achebe takes full responsibility for it. . . (Gordimer 26).

> The scenes which build up the confrontation between the despot and his two former friends are often vivid . . . Certain character sketches also come alive. . . (Pryce-Jones 1106).

Vivid scenes, "live" characters, the novel as poem—textbook gestures from reviewers who cannot, or do not want to, see the pain and outrage behind both the "mustered discipline of skill" (Gordimer 1) and the complex strategies for the preservation of hope.

Achebe himself foregrounds "telling of the story." The elder from Abazon says

> Recalling-is-Greatest. Why? Because it is only the story can continue beyond the war and the warrior. . . . It is the story, not the others, that saves our progeny from blundering like blind beggars into the spikes of the cactus fence. . . . The story is our escort;

without it, we are blind (124).

The particular "teller" that the elder has in mind, Ikem, is murdered. But his telling has sown good seed—in the student leader Emmanuel who is nobly equal to the demands of the crisis, in the taxi-driver union men, in the officer who connives at Chris Oriko's escape and is at the end a member of the group around Beatrice. We know only too well that such a group could itself be doomed—but the strategy permits a hope that the telling will remain, whether as *Anthills* itself or in some other form, to save progeny from the spikes of the cactus fence. It is clear, from the deaths of Ikem and Chris, from the precariousness of the relief from dictatorship (the precariousness is signalled by the drunken sergeant's use of the liberation spree to drag off the girl and by his shooting Chris), that the salvation cannot be from harm and death. But from corruption, evil-mindedness, loss of humanity. Making possible the hope that some clean souls at least might seek to make perfect their will.

To define the hope and suggest the possibilities in which it might be grounded—however utopian or "ideal" both might seem—Achebe brings a complex seeing and sure control of varied resources that betokens a matured art. The mode is not perhaps as immediately attractive or as persuasive as in *Things Fall Apart*. Perhaps this is because Achebe is aware of the need for tact and careful contextualization in the treatment of material far more volatile than the representation of the colonial trauma. In *Things Fall Apart* Achebe was dealing with a relatively more manageable past and attempting a pedagogy with which most readers found it easy to concur. In *Anthills* he is closer to the bone, concerned with issues and situations which could still blow up in his face.

But not fatally. The Nigeria that could be seen as mirrored in his fictive Kangan was already almost a generation past. The seeds of evil and horror remain in the current reality, giving point and necessity to Achebe's monitions, and to his tentative symbolization of the socio-spiritual order that could give his nation a future worth living (and dying) for. But it is still the case that the situation of the action in a firmly completed past (there has been a coup, the dictator has disappeared) puts the author and the more vocally appreciative of his readers out of any danger of being whisked off to torture and death like Ikem by officious vigilantes. We in Lanka are grimly aware of the possibility after the murder of journalist, poet, human rights activist Richard de Zoysa.

There is, too, for us risk of an almost opposite kind. Recently the poet Richard Murphy, a regular visitor to Lanka and an extremely sympathetic, concerned observer/participant in our troubles, observed that much of what Lankans were writing about today was too close to its occasions. The communication was intense and passionate, but perhaps too raw.

> The comment is not unfair. A story ends:
> The whole, hopeless, death-dealing duel, I thought wearily. Those were real salt tears pouring unrestrainedly now, down my cheeks to mix with the clotted blood, the traces of vomit and grime congealed upon them. And I was not ashamed (Seneviratne 63).

The narrator is an officer on patrol against terrorists in the jungles, recalling his discovery only the previous night that his uncle has been making millions running guns to the terrorists—money with which the unsuspecting officer and his friends were entertained. The story is extremely moving, the detail precisely observed, the contrasts and contradictions effectively managed—yet the note at the end is surely obtrusive, a shade too insistent.

The passionate intensity of the most powerful poetry that has come out of the current crisis in Sri Lanka—c.f. Jean Arasanayagam's *Apocalypse '83* and *Trial by Terror* and the poems of an impressive number of writers, many of them young—foreground the suffering, the disasters, the episodes of courage or compassion, of our iron time. Their rhetoric is the imagery of blood, death, dispossession and displacement and the jagged rhythms and irregular lineation that seek to present the effect of urgent, unvarnished speech:

> There is no sleep left inside my brain
> My dreams are jagged wounds streaming
> Into my eyes and the lids are open
> Like coffins. . . (Arasanayagam 21).

> A house divided
> its pillars bombed and blasted
> its stones piled over fallen rafters
> and sisters weeping over moveless corpses.
> (Wijeratne 8).

> History
> Is gashed out on this dumb street, the brand
> of Cain is hewn in ash-and-smash. . . (Ephraums 39).

> The thing lies there.
> Hugging the ripe mud
> from the ditch beside my home,
> A crisp carcass
> part cooked, part raw.
> A necklace of rubber,
> steel wire, adorns it. . . (Chandrasekera).

Sometimes a writer chooses the strategy of letting the facts speak for themselves, the authorial presence showing only in the sharpening of contrasts or juxtapositions:

> A woman drags her injured son
> In a gunny bag through the forest
> After the attack talking talking to him

He is listening through the woven deathsack
Leaking with blood. . . (Arasanayagam 20).

We blow out the kerosene lamp
And cling to each other desperately in the dark
Hold our breath
And wait for the inevitable. . . .
I feel cramped
But I don't move
For the creaking of the bed might invite
Unwelcome visitors;
Suddenly a gun cracks its verdict. . . (Jayawickrema).

A mob stops a car with four occupants "a girl, a boy/ (Between four and five it seemed) and their/ Parents—I guessed. . . ." The mob proceeds to "Action, by their routine. Pouring/Petrol. . . ." Then

. . . someone noticing something odd
As it were, opened the two left side
Doors, took away the two children, crying and resisting
As they were moved away from their parents. . . .

A match is set to the petrol and "Around/The fire they chattered";

Then suddenly the man inside
Breaking open the door, was
Out, his shirt already on
Fire and hair too. Then bending,

Took his two children . . .
Re-entered the car.

Still the ruined car

Is there, by the roadside
With other such things (B. Fernando 12-13).

Such writing has great immediacy of witness, is troubling and deeply moving in its "telling of the story" and courageous where intervention has drawn bloody reprisal or at least contempt. It is hopeful, for to speak truth at all in such days is to hope to save our progeny from the spikes of the cactus fence, abjuring the sentimental luxury of complete and speechless despair. Its risk is that it may not outlive its occasions, may even recede into a limbo of record, as tales of atavistic outrages in the process of a nation's growth to civilized maturity. Of course it may be said that this does not matter, for it will have done its work in the world.

Two distinguished Lankan responses to current reality might be brought into this account here—Rajiva Wijesinha's *Acts of Faith* and P.B. Rambukwelle's *The Desert Makers*. *Acts of Faith* could be called a black political comedy. Moral passion is given force and focus as the comedy sets up a fruitful tension between distantiation and involvement, for instance by the use of such names as Tom, Dick and Harry for the President's family and Matthew, Mark, Luke and John for the principal members of the cabinet—a cast of characters which includes a Red Shadow, a Black Shadow, Snow White and Seven Dwarfs—and the effect of extravaganza imparted by such devices as the elaborate use of TV: the cameras are always on location whether to zoom in on the underwear of the Papal Nuncio and the Red Shadow, caught on the way to the airport, or the slaughter of Luke, Snow White and the accompanying Dwarfs as the latter arrive by helicopter. The denouement is precipitated by an exquisitely detailed and inventively constructed comedy of disaster. The veteran Leninist gets himself up as Daisy Belle and visits the President with a bomb fixed up as one of 'her' breasts. When Dick attempts to paw the lady he, the Leninist and the President's wife die, setting off a sequence of grotesque plots, betrayals, murders and what have you that finally removes from the scene every one of the political characters except the President himself. This Jonsonian moral scheme is perhaps the novelist's act of faith as against the faithlessness and the corruptions of Faith of the ruling clique—the desperate hopefulness of a pessimistic patriot who sees that the country and its people have become simply the background or the material (depending on how you look at it) for the power contests of the mighty. However, the tone and content of the finale suggest that the faith is actually hopeless since we are informed of the imminence of a political marriage accompanied by symbols that "recall"—and hence predict— "imperial joys." Rajiva Wijesinha gives us innumerable shafts of incidental satire, while he has true novelistic gifts for inventive narrative and for getting inside his characters—even the totally unsavoury Matthew—and the novel is not without tenderness, pathos and heroism, particularly in those parts of it involving Harry, the episcopal brother of the President.

Central to Rambukwelle's *The Desert Makers* is another contemporary theme—the displacement of people and the destruction of traditional social complexes with their intricate structure of customs, beliefs, traditions and relationships as massive new dams and power and irrigation schemes are built in the Kandyan heartlands. The author also weaves in other themes: the validity of "modern" education, Sri Lankan style, the betrayal of trust by persons in high places—an archaeological panjandrum loots a newly excavated shrine of a priceless shoulder ornament before piously cementing the relic chamber to prevent offence to religious susceptibilities, etc.—the conflict between traditional values and new social mores. The novel ends with the self-immolation of Medduma in an act of defiance that is both tragic and exultant. This would seem a strange end to a novel that is characteristically exuberant and rich in comic invention, but it becomes evident as the narrative develops that the author is creating a kind of comedy of desperation as a mode of controlling his account of decadence. The proliferation of incident and plotlines evinces the imaginative agility of the writer, as does his very personal idiom. That idiom has been described as "consciously experimental and innovative. . . . The significant characteristics are the width of resources tapped; the adventurousness in innovation; and the innovative creativity of the style range developed" (S. Fernando 123). The style range is large, "colloquial styles interweave with acrolect. For narration, SLE acrolect is frequently inflated to a high-style" (S. Fernando 124). As an example of the former we have

> 'You know what this plant is, my friend'. . .
> 'Of course, why not, brother Baaron? Cha!
> this is our hemp plant, no?' (S. Fernando 127).

Fernando notes how "similes from domestic life bring description down to earth, 'like a louse at the bottom of a brush,'" and "local sources provide imaginative applications, 'swam into the storm like a stray cow into a ripe paddy field,'" while literary quotations, "as if the last days of Pompeii were upon the city" are as likely as imagery from modern society, "a birthday like a recurring decimal" (129).

Comparison of these novels with *Anthills*, however, reinforces one's respect for Achebe's command of his resources, explaining perhaps why this novel of unfamiliar places and people has such power over the imagination.

Achebe brings a whole country and its peoples into *Anthills* as Wijesinha does not in *Acts of Faith*. The mobs and marchers, the soldiers and servants of the latter novel remain the anonymous extras of a drama performed primarily by the highly placed, the members of the "family structures that dominate such societies" as the blurb has it. The dwarfs, the shadows remain largely fantasy-creatures, elves and goblins weaving in and out of the larger action. This focus on the power game of the mighty and the aspirant serves the author's satiric purposes, but it also accentuates the final impression of hopelessness, for the scheme has no place for new sources of energy or moral sense. It also tends to invite the reader to share a somewhat Olympian point of view, not unlike that of V.S. Naipaul in *A Bend in the River* or John Updike in *The Coup*.

Significantly, this is accompanied by the pervasive use of an idiosyncratic, acrolectal idiom, except that a comic variant is developed for Tom, the President, which adds to his general ridiculousness. At a second or third reading the impressions seem increasingly to be refracted through a, one would not say obtrusive, perhaps a marked, a distinctive authorial consciousness.

The idiom of *The Desert Makers* enriches a basically "educated Lankan English" with a wide range of effect to form a distinctive Rambukwelle poetry. The prose of *Acts of Faith* is a "language without metaphor," to use Godfrey Gunatilleke's expressive phrase. Its verve comes from larger structural features; the author's imagination typically creates situations and satiric portraits. Rambukwelle also achieves a respectable range of speech—his people are individualized by how they speak as much as by what they do. The limitation of *The Desert Makers* is closely related to its chief strength—the author's concern for his theme, and for the people, traditions and indeed actual places crunched under the tread of "development." But where the whole nation concurs with, perceives the necessity for, the dams, the new roads, the reservoirs, the new towns—and despite the displacements and heartaches—the author's concerns must seem rather those of a latter-day Romantic. The novel is a memorialization of a part of Lankan reality for which the end was inevitable: the triumphal tragedy of the end is noble and courageous, but also, viewed in the total socio-historical context, a purely gestural defiance or ceremonial suicide which cannot be related to any meaningful possibility in today's Lanka. This part of *The Desert Makers* is a moving threnody, but the suffering is of necessary change.

This could hardly be said of *Anthills*. The extended coda to the novel presents to us a grouping that prefigures a true ideal community—a real democracy—for Achebe's Nigeria, one which incorporates the taxi-drivers, the market woman, the servant, the relatives from the hinterland with the young intellectual—the student leader Emmanuel—and the mature, tested-by-tragedy Assistant Secretary for Finance Beatrice; it includes the officer. Beatrice is both English-Honours First Class, England-returned been-to, and Mother Goddess Idoto. The child of the charismatic, daring newspaper editor and poet Ikem is borne by the shop girl Elewa, daughter of a market woman.

And if we know it is ideal, a poetic invention, a metaphor for hope, it is also real, because these people have arrived together through a novel-long confluence developed with consummate tact.

Thus the taxi-drivers: they first arrive in the action in, seemingly, a totally accidental way, as peripheral local colour—one of them is the most aggressive element in a traffic jam, engaging in a battle of wills, or steering wheels, with Ikem. Their discovery of Ikem's identity a while later seems equally fortuitous, but it leads to an important clarification of the thought processes of ordinary people for Ikem, while at the same time defining *his* practical democracy and social consciousness—they are grateful for the improvement of their parking lot as a result of his journalistic intervention. They come to play a part in the campaign to whip up protest against the murder of Ikem, and their role in the escape of Chris Oriko is crucial.

Their presence in the group around Beatrice at the end, along with the provincial Adamma, Elewa who has borne Ikem's child, the relatives from Elewa's village, Elewa's market woman mother, Agatha the servant and Aina, the taxi-driver's wife, with the student leader and the sympathetic officer included, chimes in with the true import of Chris Oriko's last words, his final message.

That message, "the last green," originally thought to be "the last grin" (230-32) and so a nihilistic recognition of Absurdity, now reads as a dying political insight; that he is the last of the green bottles to fall off the wall. Sam, the dictator,

Ikem and Chris had been friends who seemed to have the fate of Kangan in their hands, the central men of power in their country, though in different ways. That they all "fall off the wall" registers Achebe's conviction, expressed in the *Kunapipi* interview with Anna Rutherford, that "the people are the owners of the country . . . anything which is not rooted in them is superficial. . ." (5). Hence the special appropriateness of the untutored Adamma being the one who heard aright (unlike Emmanuel—a potential "green bottle," already a student leader and intellectual) and of the "message" being interpreted correctly by Goddess-Muse-Beloved Beatrice at a warmly democratic gathering for the "naming" of the child of Ikem and Elewa. The child is named "May-the-path-never-close."

From the vantge point of the end, the novel hardly "shows signs of piecemeal composition and interrupted inspiration" (Updike 114). The "fractured telling" from "a multiplicity of viewpoints" and in "voices" which range from "poems and myths to cocktail gossip . . . West African patois" (Updike 114) and the London University English of the been-to is seen clearly as carefully structured to encourage in readers a seeing that is complex but also precisely articulated to suggest the "road to self-redemption" (*Anthills* 160). As James Marcus put it in his *Nation* review "Achebe establishes hope as a given, as the only conceivable response to suffering" (540).

One feature of *Anthills* is perhaps specific to the Nigerian situation, and difficult for South Asians writing in English to match. Achebe makes lavish use of Nigerian English (es?) in representing the speech of persons like Elewa, her market-woman mother, the taxi-drivers, the soldiers—members of the Nigerian urban prolctariat for whom one presumes, this is (these are?) the language(s?) of their everyday transactions. The non-Nigerian may often have to guess what some words and phrases really mean, even as he glimpses the colour and verve of the utterance. In his use of such English (as much as in his incorporation of such resonances as the Beatrice-Goddess Idoto connection or the hymn to Idemili) Achebe confidently writes a

Nigerian novel, leaving it to the users of other Englishes to come to terms with it as best as they can. Some might not: John Updike speaks of "almost unintelligible dialogue in West African patois" (114) in his *New Yorker* review, though one recalls the practice of many American writers from the days of *Huck Finn* to those of *Beloved* including the use of subcultural idioms and camp.

Not that the conditions for such achievement exist only in the U.S. or Nigeria, as Erna Brodber's analogous achievement in *Myal* might show. But for the South Asian writer the corresponding range of "voices" would include many indigenous languages and dialects for which feasible translations would have to be found—a daunting programme if the scope is to be anything like that of *Anthills*.

Achebe brings off the representation of "voices" magnificently, so that, despite all his caveats, John Updike is constrained to say,

> Life, life, persisting and seeking new combinations,
> is what emerges. . . (116).

Telling: Writing: Printing—
Orality and Achebe's Short Stories

BALA KOTHANDARAMAN

If absence cries out for presence, the in/exclusion of a consideration of Achebe's short stories among a bouquet of tributes to his narrative power raises some interesting issues in terms of narrative theory and of postcoloniality.

Achebe critics have invariably—and justifiably so—praised this writer's skill in telling a story ably and in the process making subtly, and often overtly, all the points that a sensitive Nigerian/African/postcolonial would wish to. In particular, they highlight Achebe's superb presentation of the various devices of Igbo oral narrative tradition and the resonances of spoken language which mark his contribution to the novel in English.

Novel: interestingly, critics address themselves to the features of orature among Achebe's works in this most specifically post-Gutenberg genre. Charles Nnolim likens the form and function of folklore (which he defines as the "unrecorded traditions of a people as they appear in their popular fiction, customs, belief, magic, ritual, superstitions and proverbial sayings" and which "includes myths, legends, stories, omens, charms, spells found among a homogeneous group of people" [35]) in Achebe's novels to "dormant seeds lying in the dry season earth, waiting for the rain" (35), which is itself a popular Igbo proverb. R.N. Egudu in his useful analysis, "Achebe and the Igbo Narrative Tradition," concludes that Achebe's narrative art, committed as it is to the sociocultural reality of the Igbo world, contributes to the "rehabilitation of the novel as a borrowed art form in Africa"

(53). Critics round the globe invariably highlight Achebe's skill in reflecting folklore and the oral narrative tradition in his novels; and conversely, examine the novels for these qualities as pointers of the distinctivenesss of his works.

In such a process, Achebe's short stories which might logically bear a closer relationship to the oral tradition are usually left out of the critical appraisals. The *Girls at War and Other Stories* collection is given a chapter (usually a brief one) in full-length studies of the author (as in Killam, Carroll or Innes), the dozen stories classified into a few thematic groups, and individual ones referred to episodes which they recall in some of Achebe's novels ("The Voter" and "Marriage is a Private Affair," for instance, readily recall situations in *A Man of the People* and *No Longer at Ease* with some variations).

This essay does not aim at a critical examination of Achebe's short stories, as that has been more than adequately done by the critics cited among others. Innes, for instance, makes the perceptive comment that

> Whereas the novels [i.e. the first four] have told the stories of those who aspired to be central to their communities or their nation, these stories dwell on the perspectives and situations of those who have never seen themselves as holders of power . . . [people] concerned with physical and psychological survival, a struggle in which they generally see themselves more or less lucky rather than good or clever (123).

These "marginalized people," she adds, "are given space and voice" in *Anthills of the Savannah* (133).

The thrust of this essay is to relocate Achebe's short stories in the orality/literacy polarity and in the genre criticism of the short story and thus, by extension, to critique a significant body of neglected postcolonial writing.

Almost all the major postcolonial writers, especially those

who could be termed "first-generation" (albeit in a very general way) are, or have been, practitioners of the short story. In fact, I had thought of comparing R.K. Narayan's /Mulk Raj Anand's/ Raja Rao's output in this genre to Achebe's for the South Asian perspective of the present volume. The "Big Three" of Indian Writing in English, like Achebe, are widely acclaimed as novelists. The similarity of the situation vis-à-vis other African and Commonwealth writers thereupon struck me as interesting and led to raising the kinds of questions suggested a little earlier.

In his Preface to the 1972 *Girls at War and Other Stories,* Achebe recalls that his "earliest short stories were published as long ago as twenty years in the Ibadan student magazine, *The University Herald.*" He expresses his gratitude to Professors Thomas Melone and G.D. Killam for tracking down some of the earliest ones published in this collection (in which two early stories included in the first edition were deleted by Achebe himself and a recent one, "Sugar Baby," added). Achebe's light-hearted reference to his "possible departures" into "relieved competence" and/or "relieved and unrelieved incompetence" (playing upon Soyinka's comment on the "unrelieved competence" of his [Achebe's] novels) perhaps indicates the lionized novelist's (and his critics') attitude to the short stories.

In his introduction to an anthology of African short stories, J.de Grandsaigne enumerates the possible reasons for critics' neglect of a genre which has been flourishing in the continent since the 1950s; short stories

> appear mainly in the popular press and are therefore rated very low; they serve as a means of apprenticeship in creative writing for aspiring writers, consequently earning the disparaging label of 'beginner's work'; they seem to keep very much in line with the European or western model and can then be scorned as too 'derivative' (4-5).

de Grandsaigne also cites some African writers (Alex La Guma,

Taban lo Liyong, Ama Ata Aidoo) who, like "their western counterparts" consider "the short story purely as a literary challenge." He opines that the African short story must be seen in a wider perspective as reflecting modern life, as (quoting Ulli Beier) "snapshots, revealing a terrible moment of truth," as making a social statement as much as novels do (5).

de Grandsaigne disagrees with Charles Larson's view that the modern African short story belongs to an "oral literary tradition centuries old," as well as with Gary Spackey's opinion that the contact between oral literature and the short story has been minimal (de Grandsaigne 10). His own classification of the short story is based on the distinction he makes between novel and short story, between short story and tale with the tale considered as being closer to the oral tradition and narrated with an avowed moral purpose. He considers the short story genre as making its mark in nineteenth century Europe, and invokes Edgar Allan Poe's "rules governing its composition" (as critics of the genre invariably do).

So with Achebe critics examining the "oral tradition" in the novels and the editor of a pedagogical anthology of African short stories preferring to place the short story in a postliterate, Euro-derived mode, it might be useful to make interventions invoking both short story criticism and the "oral literary" tradition.

Ian Reid's compact (and wide-ranging) book *The Short Story* for the *Critical Idiom* series is divided into "Problems of definition," "Growth of a genre," "Tributary forms," "Brevity expanded," and "Essential qualities?" (which examines Poe's postulates). Reid points out that the term "short story," "designating a particular kind of literary product, gained formal admittance into the vocabulary of English readers" (1) only in 1933; although the form itself has been conspicuous over the last 150 years in the literature of several countries. Critical attention, he adds, is not commensurate with the importance of the form, a point repeated in the essays comprising a special number (Spring 1982) of *Modern Fiction Studies.* Contributors cite

Charles May's *Short Story Theories* (1976) as the best critical/theoretical anthology to date. Finding that "short story critics have traveled alone, their critical paths often crossing but rarely converging," Lohafer and Clarey bring them together in a significant 1989 publication, Lohafer herself having earlier "traveled alone" with her substantial *Coming to Terms with the Short Story* (1983).

While these scholars (and the works of others cited in the respective bibliographies) contribute immensely to the consolidation and the advancement of critical perceptions of the state of the art, the site of debate remains Euro-American, Short story writers in English and other European languages from the former colonies or immigrant/settler writers of non-Euro-American ethnic backgrounds are conspicuous by their exclusion. Would this imply that postcolonialist/Third World/ Commonwealth short story writers and critics have to swing into action to reapproriate lost spaces, to voice marginalised cultural concerns? This is among the interesting theoretical issues which provoked this essay. (The possibilities of feminist, Marxist, Black, ethnic, nationalist, and crosscultural sub-texts are, of course, inherent in the enterprise).

Cultural critiquing of world literature in English leads sometimes to an almost programmatic hunt for ethnic inheritance in contemporary works. This in turn leads, often unwittingly, to a fairly romanticized exaltation of lost, or rapidly disappearing, indigenous traditions. The critical anxiety to catch echoes of "oral tradition" and "oral literature" in postcolonial writing reflects this practice.

Walter J. Ong, pointing out the contradictory nature of the term "oral literature," distinguishes between the "primary orality" of a culture "totally untouched by any knowledge of writing or print" and the "secondary orality" of "present-day high-technology culture" wherein electronic devices which "depend for their existences and functioning" on writing and printing present a new orality (11). Ong's observation that primary oral culture in the strict sense hardly exists in the present times although "many cultures and sub-cultures, even in a high-technology ambience, preserve much of the mind-set of primary orality" (11) in varying degrees helps to place the question of "oral tradition" found in postcolonial literatures in a clearer perspective. Scholarly approaches that start with a "subsequent secondary phenomenon and par[e] away the differences" in dealing with oral literature, he remarks, often result in "serious and disabling distortion" while describing a primary phenomenon (13).

Critics of modern African literature, as mentioned earlier in this essay, tend to romanticize their recognition of the primary phenomenon in the secondary. What is necessary is to look at short stories, and other postcolonial literatures as written works emerging from cultures in which the range of orality from the primary to the secondary is prevalent in layers of accretion far more prismatic than in cultures where the vestiges of primary orality have almost completely disappeared.

Critical appraisal of the short story can thereby be given its due place in the mode of written literature; considering that the genre itself is a comparatively young one and criticism of it even more recent, the short stories of postcolonial writers should be considered part of the entire field rather than relegated to a separate space. Ian Reid urges the importance of critical awareness of the intricate process of framing narrative texts vis-à-vis particular acts of reading (especially of the short story) so as to free interpretation from the dangers of restrictiveness and distortion (Lohafer and Clarey 299). He identifies four such frames—the circumtextual, intratextual, intertextual, and extratextual—and argues for attentive adjustment to other framing possibilities. It would certainly be rewarding to consider such possibilities with Achebe's short stories and those of other postcolonial writers.

Achebe across Cultural Contexts

FEROZA JUSSAWALLA

In his essay, "The Novelist as Teacher," collected both in *Morning Yet on Creation Day* and in *Hopes and Impediments,* Achebe recalls that a student wrote him to say that he, Achebe, "had neglected to include questions and answers at the end of *Things Fall Apart* and could I make these available to him to ensure his success in next year's school certificate examination" (*Morning* 43). Like the student Achebe writes about, my first introduction to Achebe was a study of *Things Fall Apart* for my Senior Cambridge exam in November of 1968. In looking back at that question paper, which for some reason I had saved as opposed to all the other things that were abandoned in India, I am struck by the early canonization of that work. It was only ten years after the publication of the novel and *Things Fall Apart* was in the company of such works as Trollope's *Barchester Towers* and Austen's *Pride and Prejudice.* Why, I can't help wondering, was not Narayan's *Swami and Friends* or Raja Rao's *Kanthapura* on the syllabus? When I took this peculiar high school graduation exam, it was still the Senior Cambridge exam, and the question papers still came from the University of Cambridge Local Examinations Syndicate, currently quite popularized by the Inspector Morse mystery on the Public Broadcasting service, a mystery that evolves around a syndicate official selling questions to the Saudis. In his essay, "What do African Intellectuals Read?" Achebe describes this exam: "If they [students in colonial Africa or India] were offered Literature in their Cambridge School Certificate, then they probably read a couple of novels like *Pride and Prejudice, Wuthering Heights, Far Away and Long Ago,* one Shakespeare play, most likely *Julius Caesar* or *Romeo and Juliet,* and that would be all" (*Morning* 39). But as I look at this question paper, I am reminded of the caution my Indian-Christian high school teacher had imparted, "Dear, don't write about Achebe," she had said. "They will think we are incapable of writing about *Macbeth* or *Pride and Prejudice.* Those questions are only for the Africans, because they insist on being represented. We must show that we can write about English things!" Mrs. Jacobs's caution remains in my mind as the summary of the Indian response to colonialism; the African response has of course been much more militant, not quite so docilely accepting of the white man's superiority. It reminds me of the story that Indian elephants are much easier to train to work on tea estates than are African elephants, and it also reminds me of the Gikuyu proverb that when elephants fight, it is the grass that gets trampled underneath.

Achebe himself has addressed this complicated response on the part of the colonial subject, but Achebe's response also shows how the Africans had gotten beyond the "let's be more British than the British and thus show them" response of the Indians. In the essay "The Novelist as Teacher," which follows "What Do African Intellectuals Read?" in *Morning Yet on Creation Day*, he gives us two examples. One is that of his wife who while teaching English in a boys' school, asked a pupil why he wrote about winter when he meant the harmattan. "He said the other boys would call him a bushman if he did such a thing!" The other is of how the early Christian Africans of his father's day preferred to perform the Maypole dance rather than their own Nigerian dances on festival days. Of this Achebe says,

> Needless to say, we do have our own sins and blasphemies recorded against our name. If I were God, I would regard as the very worst our acceptance—for whatever reason—of racial inferiority. It is too late in the day to get worked up about it or to blame others,

> much as they may deserve such blame and condemnation. What we need to do is to look back and try and find out where we went wrong, where the rain began to beat us (*Morning* 44).

After many years of graduate education and after a heightened awareness of how I had internalized the "colonial oppressor," an incident in one of my freshman classes took me back to the colonialism of education that I myself had been raised with. A freshman Hispanic student, recognized by all her teachers as having exceptional and above freshman level abilities, objected to my teaching a novel by the Hispanic-American writer, Rudolfo Anaya, entitled *Bless Me, Ultima.* The objections were largely to his use of English intermixed with Spanish, (what linguists would call code-switching and code-mixing) but also to his use of a Chicano English. "Why are we reading this novel?" she asked me. "It is not written in good English"—a phrase I had not heard since I left India. "This English is bastardized, what we call 'pocho'," she insisted. "Plus all this stuff about old-fashioned superstitions is not what I came to university to learn about. I was hoping you would choose some great works of English literature." Here was a true colonial subject raised in a part of the world that had experienced no formal colonialism except perhaps a passing Spanish colonialism, unless of course you grant the colonialism of the white man's culture in the U.S. Southwest.

Rudolfo Acuna in *Occupied America: The Chicano's Struggle Toward Liberation* writes about the forms of colonization in America:

> At the very core of Americanization is the compelling necessity for Anglo-Americans to remake the unassimilable masses so they can be more acceptable. This is accomplished by erasing their culture, language, and values, and replacing them with Anglo-American culture, language and values. It is a

> process that has caused considerable cultural conflict for the Chicano and that has resulted in the following: many Chicanos developing negative images, many Chicanos accepting the values of the colonizers and rejecting their own heritage (146).

As we know so well, this was true of South Asia and of the many colonized nations on the continent of Africa. This then was the shared experience of colonialism and the response to colonialism that tied such diverse groups as Indians, Nigerians, Kenyans (witness the work of Ngugi wa Thiong'o) and the U.S. minorities together.

The experience with my student alerted me to the experiences of colonialism and cultural and linguistic imperialism that we as Indians in South Asia have shared, not just with other parts of the world that were the British Empire but with such colonized and marginalized peoples as the minorities in North America, some of whom are of South Asian origin. So together with Achebe I would say, "Here then is an adequate revolution for me to expose—to help my society regain belief in itself and put away the complexes of the years of denigration and self-abasement. And it is essentially a question of education, in the best sense of that word. Here I think, my aims and the deepest aspirations of my society meet" (*Morning* 44).

Of course, the common denigration of native cultures is part of the shared experience of colonization, not only of the geographical areas that made up the British Empire but also of all those peoples deemed inferior to the white man on all the various continents. When I interviewed Achebe in New York,[1] he again emphasized that one of the "worst consequences of colonization [is] that one is utterly alienated from his community." My young Hispanic student without having known it expressed the quintessence of Macaulay's minute on British education in India:

> It may be that the public mind of India may expand

> under our system till it has outgrown that system; that by good government we may educate our subjects into a capacity for better government; that, having become instructed in European knowledge, they may, in some future age, demand European institutions. Whether such a day will ever come, I know not. But never will I attempt to retard it. Whenever it comes, it will be the proudest day in English history. To have found a great people sunk in the lowest depths of slavery and superstition, to have so ruled them as to have made them desirous and capable of all the privileges of citizens, would indeed be a title to glory all our own. The sceptre may pass away from us. . . . But there are triumphs which are followed by no reverse. There is an empire exempt from all natural causes of decay. Those triumphs are the pacific triumphs of reason over barbarism; that empire is the imperishable empire of our arts and our morals, our literature and our laws (Macaulay 3).

But into this large plan of course was built the use and strength of English:

> We have to educate a people who cannot at present be educated by means of their mother tongue. . . . The claims of our language it is hardly necessary to recapitulate. . . (3).

With a missionary's belief in the power of English, the colonizers imposed the language on all those peoples deemed inferior because they did not know the language.

Thus in my teaching I have brought the commonality of the colonial experience and the use of English by South Asians and Africans to my Hispanic students. The most important common factor of course is and has been "linguistic imperialism." And Achebe, while admitting what South Asians on the Subcontinent have always admitted, that the English language gave us a way of communicating among ourselves, has also asserted (as Raja Rao did) that one had to modify English to convey our own sensibility rather than let oneself be bought over by the language and thought process of one's education. In "The African Writer and the English Language," Achebe writes of English: "If it failed to give them a song, it at least gave them [Africans] a tongue, for sighing" (*Morning* 57). But to this he adds,

> *Can he [the African writer] ever learn to use it like a native speaker?* I should say, I hope not. It is neither necessary nor desirable for him to be able to do so. The price a world language must be prepared to pay is submission to many different kinds of use. The African writer should aim to use English in a way that brings out his message best without altering the language to the extent that its value as a medium of international exchange will be lost. He should aim at fashioning out an English which is at once universal and able to carry his peculiar experience. I have in mind here the writer who has something new, something different to say (*Morning* 61).

The idea that a varied English is an important way in which a writer expresses his freedom from oppression was one that I had to convey to my "supposedly" bright Hispanic student who had, like my high school teacher, absorbed the idea that one had to be, so to speak, "more British than the British" to prove one's acceptability. This was a question that many of my bilingual-bicultural Hispanic students had to deal with. Was the English they spoke legitimate? How should they use English in their conversation and in their writing?

As a first-year lecturer, I was still working on my dissertation. The more freshman student papers I read at the University of Texas at E1 Paso—a public university located on the U.S.-Mexican border, with a 64% bilingual student population—the more I began to be acutely aware of bilingual writing in English. The parallels between what my students were saying about bilingual writing in English and the ways in which they were struggling with writing in English and what had been said by Indian and African writers about writing in English began to be an important preoccupation in my teaching and my research writing. Thus it is that both my research and my teaching took on as their prime interest the use of English in multicultural contexts. And this became one South Asian's response to using Achebe in the American classroom. Struggling with whether and how to use English for his purposes, Achebe has much to say to my students. He too makes the connection between the African and the black American experience with English by quoting from James Baldwin. Baldwin wrote,

> My quarrel with the English language has been that the language reflected none of my experience. But now I began to see the matter another way. . . . Perhaps the language was not my own because I had never attempted to use it, had only learned to imitate it (*Morning* 84).

I often pass this tenet on to my students.

While the use of literature in the composition classroom has been resisted in some teaching circles, in what I've described above, World Literature written in English fulfills an extremely useful role. It helps the student find himself among a community of other writers who have had to struggle with finding their voice in English. These writers include the Indian writers R.K. Narayan and Raja Rao, the Nigerian writers Amos Tutuola and Chinua Achebe, and the Southwestern U.S. writers Rudolfo Anaya and Leslie Marmon Silko. And a work like *Morning Yet on Creation Day* shows that these authors have also discussed in expository works their struggle with expressing themselves in the English language versus being read for wider communicability.

First of all, reading novels by authors such as Achebe helps our students, whether bilingual minority students in America or multilingual students in India, feel comfortable with expressing themselves in the English language *as they know it.* As they see the innovative ways in which the English language has been used by different authors, they begin to get over their own writing apprehension. They begin to find the appropriate voice for their personal experience. They also begin to understand the phenomenon of languages in contact—again, an experience common not just to South Asians and Africans but also to Americans.

As they begin to evaluate the efficacy of the literary works, students become aware of the difference between the "personal" voice and the "transactional" voice or the style used when communicating with a wide international audience.[2] They begin to see that a work like Tutuola's *The Palm Wine Drinkard* uses the personal voice in its entirety while a work like R.K. Narayan's *Swami and Friends* or Achebe's *Things Fall Apart* alternates between the transactional voice in the narrative and the personal, expressive voice of the characters. This raises for students the issue of the communicability of the personal, expressive voice and for them is an important step in the direction of transactional writing. It makes them aware of the need for "modulating" the writer's voice based on audience, acceptability, and appropriateness. For instance, Tutuola's *The Palm Wine Drinkard* appeals to a limited audience because it is expressed in a purely personal voice. Even Achebe, perhaps with Tutuola in mind, wrote that the African writer should "use English in a way that brings out his message best without altering the language to the extent that its value as a medium of international exchange will be lost" (*Morning* 82). Narayan's narration is transactional as it interacts with an audience in an attempt to communicate information. With simple ease Narayan in *Swami and Friends* communicates both in standard English and in Indian English. For example:

> Father was apparently deaf to Swaminathan's remarks. He stood over Swaminathan and set him to dust his books and clean his table. Swaminathan vigorously started blowing off the dust from the book covers. He caught the spider carefully, and took it to the window to throw it out. He held it outside the window and watched it for a while. It was swinging from a strand that gleamed in a hundred delicate tints (83-84).

Immediately after this, Narayan gives us the English of India:

> '*Look sharp!* Do you want a whole day to throw out the spider?' father asked . . .
>
> 'Get a piece of cloth, boy' (84).

Swami goes to his grandmother with this:

> 'Granny, get me a piece of cloth, quick!'
>
> 'Where am I *to go for a piece of cloth*?'
>
> 'Where *am I to go*?' he asked peevishly. . . .
>
> He almost wept as he said: 'I don't know what Rajam and Mani will think, *waiting for me there, if I keep on fooling here*. [This is a continuous participial construction typical of Indian English.] Granny, if Father cannot find any work to do, why shouldn't he *go and sleep*?' [rather than 'go to sleep'] (84-85). [Italics indicate localized or nativized usage.]

While many American students may have some trouble understanding the way Swami is speaking English, they can discern in such an example both a sense of "their right to their own language" and the contexts in which this language is appropriate. For Swaminathan, an anglicized, Christian mission school student in the situation of conversing with his grandmother who at best speaks some broken English, his own language is appropriate.

In "The African Writer, and the English Language," an essay reprinted in *Morning Yet on Creation Day*, Achebe gives us a similar example except that he shows us how he could have put the same passage into standard English himself. Here is the passage he cites from *Arrow of God:*

> I want one of my sons to join these people and be my eyes there. If there is nothing in it you will come back. But if there is something there you will bring home my share. The world is like a Mask, dancing. If you want to see it well you do not stand in one place. My spirit tells me those who do not befriend the white man today will be saying *had we known* tomorrow.

Immediately after this passage Achebe gives us the same passage in what might have been standard English together with his explanation of why he phrased the passage originally the way he did:

> I am sending you as a representative among these people—just to be on the safe side in case the new religion develops. One has to move with the times or else one is left behind. I have a hunch that those who fail to come to terms with the white man may well regret their lack of foresight.

To this Achebe adds, "the material is the same. But the form of the one is in character and the other is not. It is largely a matter of instinct, but judgement comes into it too" (*Morning* 61-62).

In *A Man of the People* Achebe shows how using different varieties of the English language becomes a political device and even a persuasive device. Chief Nanga, the "man of the people," finds that speaking to different people with their level or type of usage wins him popularity. With the Americans (this is now post-independence Nigeria), he speaks American English, with Odili and his "gang" a type of familiar "pidgin," and with the villagers he uses a proverbial style which we are to assume is a transliteration into English of the traditional Igbo style. In my interview with Achebe I asked him about this:

F.J.: I have to say my all-time favourite character of yours is Chief Nanga [in *A Man of the People*], primarily because of the language that he uses. I realize that at the end we're saying this man's a thoroughly corrupt person, but the way in which he can use a straightforward English in conversations maybe with Americans, and then switch to a proverbial and an African style when he's talking with Odili, and then when he's talking with the people, the way in which he can switch into pidgin and out is very important to his communicability. The various language switches are very complex. He's a great rhetor in terms of persuasion and argumention.

Achebe: He's very important. He's the only character who has the title of the book named for him. *A Man of the People* is him in a way that no other character—maybe Ezeulu in *Arrow of God,* but not the same way—is in the title. So, yes, he's a very important character; and he is proficient. He knows what he wants to do, and he's prepared to do it and has the training, the historical preparation for it. This is in part, perhaps, the tragedy of our situation. Here indeed he's this proficient, and yet he's applying it all to destroy the society. He's not applying it as Ezeulu is to save the system. He's applying it in a very narrow, selfish way. This may be the worst consequence of colonization—that one is utterly alienated from his community. The leader is not a leader of his people. He's something totally outlandish in terms of the interests, the concerns, the comfort of his people. And one can see how that came about as a consequence of the colonial system, the creation of a ruler who had no responsibility to his people. The colonialist wants somebody who can run this foreign, this alien institution, help him run it for the advantage of the colonial power. So I think that derailment, that separation of the leader from those he leads, is perhaps the greatest evil.

F.J.: Can I go into a language issue? I get frustrated over and over again whenever I see a review of *Anthills of the Savannah* which says, "I can't understand this pidgin; I can't understand this language experimentation." How do you feel? You're obviously very adept and very skilled—certainly from *A Man of the People* on—at using all the levels of language and the way in which language works in all our postcolonial societies—code-switching back and forth, translating from an African proverb, transliterating, as well as using the pidgin with the standard English in your own very beautiful English. I'm trying to come to grips with this in the sense that some people feel that pidgin should not be in African literature at all because it's not a relevant language. "Why should that be; why shouldn't that be rendered in say Gikuyu or Igbo or Hausa?" How do you feel? What are you thinking when you are developing style and language experimentation?

Achebe: I think again we're dealing with these people

who are irritating in their "this cannot be; this must not be; this will not be." I mean, why, why, why are people so frightened of letting things that happen in real life happen in literature? Pidgin exists. You talk about those who are irritated by it. There are others on the other extreme who say everything must be written in pidgin; this is our language. There are people who are saying that and it's just as absurd. Pidgin English is there.

F.J.: Is pidgin the right term for it? Is it Nigerian English, should we say?

Achebe: Well, I don't know. No, it's not Nigerian English because it's just one form of Nigerian English. It's not Creole either. If we don't like the word pidgin—and I don't like it; I don't know how it started—it's not a very good word I don't think, but we know what we're saying. But if somebody comes up with a better name for it, I'll be quite happy to adopt it. But this is what it's called. This is what it's called in Nigeria. We say, "they talk pidgin." It's there, and it's a valid language with its uses. It's used in Nigerian society in the same way as I reflect in my modern novels. There are things which it cannot do very well. There are things which it can do very well. People think it's rather inefficient, but there are even moments when it is more concise and far more efficient than Standard English.

By focusing on such language issues, American students learn a great deal not only about African culture, politics and history, but also about their own sociolinguistic situation. Similarly, Indian students discover in Achebe's handling of English a shared experience of colonialism and also a shared experience of rejection based on language. Students can thus learn how to choose an appropriate voice based on the task at hand. Achebe once said of Tutuola's fiction, "A good instinct has turned his apparent limitation in language into a weapon of great strength—a half strange dialect that serves him perfectly in the evocation of his bizarre world" (*Morning* 82). Students can thus see that in certain situations, despite colonialist rejection, their medium may be valid, and in other situations it may not be. Watching how a writer varies the various styles he has at his disposal sets an important example for students whether in South Asia, Africa or the United States.

I believe that the introduction of cross-cultural literature in the English composition classroom, whether as English composition in high school or as General English at the college level, also fulfils two related goals: those of cognitive development and of cultural literacy. It not only teaches students about the way language is used by writers who have experiences similar to theirs but it also makes them more accepting of cultural diversity. The use of cross-cultural literature provides concrete direction for such work in cognitive development. It challenges the student who says, "I am monocultural and want my world to remain so," as much as it challenges the student who says, "I don't care about the way English is spoken in India, Nigeria, or anywhere else." Above all it raises their awareness of the process of colonization and the ways in which some of the psychological domination of colonialism can be resisted—ways, as Ngugi would say, of "decolonising the mind."

NOTES

1. Bapsy Sidhwa most kindly arranged the interview with Achebe in New York.
2. "Personal voice" and "transactional voice" are terms used by composition specialists in America when referring to a student writing in his/her own voice and when the student is writing to interact with an audience in a more "formal" voice.

Achebe and the Indians

BERNTH LINDFORS

From September through mid-December of 1989 I conducted research in India on the teaching of non-British literatures in English departments at Indian universities. I was curious to know to what extent the so-called "new literatures in English" were being taught and studied—not just Third World anglophone literatures from Africa, the Caribbean and South Asia (most notably from India itself) but also the not-so-new First World literatures from Canada, Australia, New Zealand, and even the United States of America. To put it another way, I wanted to find out how far university English studies in India, a former British colony, had been decolonized since independence. How much of the rest of the English-speaking world was now visible in the literature curriculum? Which authors and which texts from outside the traditional English canon were being read? And how seriously were they being studied? Did the courses in which they were covered make up part of the programme of work required of all undergraduate and post-graduate students, or were such courses relegated to the status of exotic options available to whoever might wish to venture a bit beyond the mainstream syllabus? Did non-British literatures command as much respect in Indian universities as British literature ?

I had done a similar survey of curricular change in anglophone Africa three years earlier, examining the degree to which African literature had been accommodated in English programmes at 40 universities in 14 independent nations. The results of that study showed that African literature was being taught on nearly all the campuses surveyed (the University of Mauritius being the only exception), and that in a few places it had achieved paramountcy, figuring in fifty percent or more of the courses required for a literature degree. In most undergraduate programmes, however, British literature still got the lion's share of attention. North American literature, especially its Afro-American and Afro-Caribbean offshoots, had made striking gains here and there, but the literary output of the remainder of the English-speaking world (India, Canada, Australia, New Zealand, Singapore, and the South Pacific islands) had been granted almost no recognition at all, being virtually ignored in even the most innovative programmes. The tendency was for African and other black literatures to drive out some of the British literature but never to rout it completely. Many English departments claimed to be aiming at a balanced curriculum, one that exposed students to the classic British authors (Shakespeare, Dickens and the rest) as well as to the best contemporary African writers, but there was little agreement on what constituted the ideal mix. One programme's balance was another programme's disequilibrium. The winds of curricular change were still blowing across the African continent, so the dust hadn't quite settled yet.

In India, on the other hand, the opening up of the English curriculum to non-British subject matter had been a slower and more orderly process. It had proceeded in three distinct phases, with American literature, aided by a postwar infusion of Fulbright funds for teaching and research, infiltrating the syllabus in a significant way in the 1950s, then Indian literature in English gaining a secure academic foothold about a decade later, and finally "Commonwealth Literature" (by which was meant the literatures of the rest of the English-speaking world) earning a small niche for itself only as recently as the 1970s and 1980s. But not all English programmes in the nation were affected by these changes in the same way. Today there are still some English departments at Indian Universities that teach only British literature, others that teach mainly British literature with a small admixture of American and Indian literatures, and yet others that offer courses in American, Indian and Commonwealth literatures only at the post-graduate level. In fact, the great majority of English programmes at Indian universities remain steadfastly Anglocentric, elevating British literature above all others and tolerating little substantive deviation from the type of curriculum that existed during colonial times. Some of these fossilized programmes appear to have resisted or effectively deflected the winds of change. Unlike their counterparts in anglophone Africa, most university English departments in India have not undergone a major curricular revolution. Britannia still rules the syllabus.

But in those institutions where there has been change, that change has been broader and more truly international than in Africa. This larger vision is reflected in other ways as well. For instance, there is so lively an interest in Australian literature in India today that an *Indian Journal of Australian Studies* has been launched. There are also at least half a dozen journals devoted almost entirely to Commonwealth literature, three of which—*The Literary Criterion, The Literary Half-Yearly,* and *Commonwealth Quarterly*—have been published in one city, Mysore in south India, for an average of twenty years or more. Yet another journal is *The Commonwealth Review*, a biannual brought out by the Indian Society for Commonwealth Studies. Academic conferences are held periodically on African, Caribbean, Canadian, Australian and New Zealand literatures as well as on Commonwealth literature, and professional scholarly bodies have sprung up to cater to the interests of researchers specializing in one or more of these new literatures in English. In addition, American literature has continued to receive a great deal of serious scholarly attention, and Indian literature in English has gradually emerged as a major new literary discipline in the Indian academic world. In short, in those places in India where curricular or extracurricular innovation has occurred, there has been a noticeably greater literary consmopolitanism than in Africa. Indian scholars interested in the wider world of English studies tend to look outward as much as they look inward; they are not entirely preoccupied with local matters.

Of course, such cosmopolitanism can have its hazards. It is difficult for any individual, no matter how industrious, to gain a thorough mastery of half a dozen national literatures and of the distinctive cultures from which they have emerged. This difficulty is compounded when, as in India, there is a serious shortage of primary and secondary texts published abroad. A scholar with limited access to such vital resources is not likely to become an authority in his field, especially if that field consists of several large subplots widely separated in time and space and forever in need of attentive cultivation. By attempting to stretch himself thin over such distant territories and to work without adequate tools, the Commonwealth literature scholar in India runs the risk of becoming a jack of all anglophone literatures and a master of none.

But despite such obstacles, despite such hazards, there exists among the most broadminded of Indian scholars a lively curiosity about new literary phenomena elsewhere and a readiness to move circumspectly into Third World regions where orthodox Anglophiles fear to tread. A little knowledge may be a dangerous thing, but it can also be a delightful thing, leading to insights that otherwise might never occur to a mind devoid of such knowledge. A number of adventurous Indian scholars have been willing to take the risks attendant upon exploring unfamiliar African literary landscapes, and their gambles have paid off not only for themselves but also for others who have been exposed to the new ideas these scholars have generated and disseminated. By venturing rather far afield, they have made fresh discoveries that have helped to draw India and Africa much closer together intellectually.

Before looking at a few examples of their work, it may be well to say a few words about how African literature is taught at Indian universities, for the demands of teaching may influence or even determine the supply of scholarship in a given area, especially a brand-new area. In India, African literature usually is taught as a component in courses on Commonwealth literature. Out of 66 Indian university English departments that responded to a questionnaire sent to 110 institutions eliciting information about current teaching practices, only three reported offering a separate course on African literature, and in one of these, the coverage of Africa was combined with coverage of literature from the West Indies. A few departments taught representative African texts in courses on "Post-colonial Literature," "The New Literatures in English" and "Modern Fiction," but the large majority (25 of the 33 that fielded such new courses) subsumed African literature under the umbrella of "Commonwealth Literature." One practical consequence of this absorption was that only a few African works were being read in these courses—usually two or three at the most but sometimes merely a single text. Judging from the sample of responses received, one could conclude that half (i.e., 33 of the 66 respondents) of the university English departments in India now offer at least one course on the new literatures in English but that the African component of such courses is quite small, though perhaps no smaller than that of any other area of the Commonwealth.

What does an Indian teacher of a course on Commonwealth literature do when confronted with the problem of selecting one or two texts to represent the literary output of the entire African continent? From the evidence now in hand, the answer is clear: teach Achebe. If there is extra time, teach Soyinka too and then perhaps Ngugi and a few poets, but start with the most important writer and the most significant single text. Start with Achebe. Start with *Things Fall Apart*. Achebe's works were taught in 37 courses at 32 of the 33 institutions in India that reported offering courses in new literatures in English. *Things Fall Apart* was the text selected in 24 of these courses, *Arrow of God* and *No Longer at Ease* were chosen in 3 courses each, *A Man of the People* was used in 2 courses, and selections from Achebe's poetry and short stories were assigned in 3 courses.

In comparison, Soyinka's works were required reading in

28 courses at 25 institutions, but there was no consensus on which of his works was most important. *The Road* was used in 11 courses, *A Dance of the Forests* in 6, *The Lion and the Jewel* in 3, and *The Interpreters, Kongi's Harvest* and *Death and the King's Horseman* in 2 each. Ngugi's works were assigned in only 10 courses at 9 institutions: *Homecoming* and *A Grain of Wheat* in 2 courses each, and *The River Between, Weep Not, Child, Devil on the Cross,* and *Decolonizing the Mind* in one course each. Other authors occasionally read in Indian university English courses included Okigbo and Okara in 3 courses each, Armah and Clark in 2 each, and Awoonor, Brutus, Coetzee, Gordimer, La Guma, Paton, Peters and Rubadiri in one each. These statistics prove very clearly that Achebe is the African author most frequently taught and that *Things Fall Apart* is the African text most widely read at these institutions. Most Indian students are introduced to African literature through Achebe, and for some of them African literature begins and ends with *Things Fall Apart*.

The same pattern holds in Indian scholarship on African literature. Although there have been occasional essays covering such writers as Abrahams, Amadi, Brutus, Clark, Egbuna, Mphahlele, Mwangi, Nwankwo, Nwapa, Okara, Okigbo, p'Bitek, Rubadiri, Ruganda and Tutuola, most attention has focused on the big three: Achebe, Soyinka, and to a far lesser extent, Ngugi. Moreover, the interest in Soyinka and Ngugi is relatively recent, but discussion of Achebe's work goes back a full quarter of a century. Again, as can be seen in the bibliography attached to this paper, the bulk of the commentary on Achebe has dealt with *Things Fall Apart,* the book Indian teachers and students know best.

Indian scholars have adopted a variety of approaches to Achebe's writing. One favourite tactic is to compare his themes and techniques to those employed by writers from India and other Third World countries. Ahmed Ali, R.K. Narayan, Raja Rao, Mulk Raj Anand, Kamala Markandaya, V.S. Naipaul, George Lamming and Gabriel Garcia Marquez have been singled out for comparisons of this kind. So have certain African and Afro-American writers, namely Cyprian Ekwensi, T.M. Aluko, Ngugi wa Thiong'o, Richard Wright, Ralph Ellison and James Baldwin. The comparative approach has the double advantage of setting Achebe's achievements in a larger context of literary creativity and simultaneously providing a sufficiently limited number of points of reference for meaningful indepth analysis. The critic can thus study Achebe both from a distance and close up by rubbing him against his peers and observing where the side-by-side contacts yield the greatest sparks of insight. The results sometimes can be quite illuminating.

Another variety of scholarship favoured by Indian academics is close reading of the sort commonly referred to as "New Criticism." This approach, no longer new, focuses on the text alone, exploring aspects of its texture and avoiding any examination of its social and political context. This is a safe mode of entry into African literature for readers who have never been to Africa and therefore cannot speak with any confidence about the particular environment out of which a work has emerged. By concentrating on the word rather than on the world behind the work, they can attempt to come to terms with aesthetic dimensions of a literary text. They are concerned almost exclusively with verbal artistry.

A third approach adopted by Indian scholars who write about Achebe is a kind of thematic explication that deals primarily with the subjects, issues and ideas that animate Achebe's writing. In such criticism the background of the author or a text may be foregrounded to explain the situation or predicament in real life that appears to have inspired the literary work. Here biographical, historical, sociological or economic factors may play a significant role in the analysis, but sometimes these contextualizing phenomena may be extrapolated or intuited from the text rather than from a close investigation of the life and times of the author.

Of course, in India, as in other parts of the world where Achebe's works are discussed, different interpretations of the same literary data do arise. There has been at least one good academic fistfight in Indian journals concerning the significance in *Things Fall Apart* of the death of Okoli, a minor character in the Christian community in Mbanta who is alleged to have killed the sacred python (see the articles by Dipak Pal and Bala Kothandaraman). The vigour and persuasiveness of argumentation in this debate reveal an intelligent attentiveness to the text that bodes well for African literature studies in India. If nothing else, it shows that critics there do care about what they read and sometimes care passionately enough to quarrel about subtle points of interpretation. And this is done in classic contestatory style, an energetic mode of debate sufficiently blunt and forceful to undercut the common notion of Indians as a nonviolent people!

In fact, there is nothing in Indian criticism of Achebe and his works that sets it apart from criticism being done elsewhere. Indian critics have been drawn to formal and contextual issues just as critics in other parts of the world have been. They have also made productive use of whatever secondary sources they have found available, though their range of reference, particularly to journals and books published in Africa, may not be as wide as that of scholars who have access to fuller university libraries. Nonetheless, they are quite serious about what they do, and their appraisals of matters that touch close to home—topics such as Achebe's handling of colonialism, nationalism, ethnicity, religion, culture conflict, and stylistic innovation in a second language—frequently are insightful and well-informed. They bring another Third World perspective to bear on Achebe's works, a perspective shaped to some degree by similar Third World historical and cross-cultural experience. In certain important ways they are closer to their subject than European and American critics are.

There are also a few Indian critics who operate from a base outside India—some of them (such as Uma Parameswaran in Canada, P.D. Tripathi in Zambia, and Eira Patnaik in the United States of America) temporarily or permanently teaching abroad, others (such as Abdul JanMohamed, Peter Nazareth and Bahadur Tejani, all of whom are East African Asians by origin) having migrated from one location in the Indian diaspora to another (JanMohamed and Nazareth to the USA, Tejani to Nigeria). These peripatetic scholars have increased international awareness of Achebe's writing by publishing articles and books in whatever part of the world they happen to inhabit. JanMohamed's commentaries are particularly noteworthy as sophisticated contributions to contemporary literary theory; his *Manichean Aesthetics* is one of the best theoretical works written on African literature.

Another group of scholars who should not be ignored in this survey are the translators. Translations of samples of Achebe's writing have appeared in at least six Indian languages. *Things Fall Apart* has been published in its entirety in Punjabi; extracts from Achebe's poetry and criticism have been anthologized in Tamil; an extract from his fiction has been anthologized in Telugu; several of his short stories have appeared in Hindi journals and newspapers; and one cultural magazine called *Pustaka Prapancha,* which is published in the Kannada language, has devoted an entire issue to commentary on and translations of examples of Achebe's work. I doubt that any other African author has been made available to the South Asian reading public in so many Indian languages. To top it all off, there is a separate English edition of *Things Fall Apart* published and distributed locally by Allied Publishers, which has branch offices in eight of India's largest cities.

Why is Achebe so popular in India? I suspect it is for much the same reason that he is popular elsewhere: his books are a pleasure—a very deep pleasure—to read. As one Indian critic put it when commenting on his first novel:

> *Things Fall Apart* appears to have been able to cast its spell on readers all the world over principally because of Achebe's seemingly artless but really dexterous handling of a theme which is essentially

> local and limited in nature but assumes perennial relevance and universal significance (Gupta 55).

Seemingly artless, really dexterous, essentially local and limited in nature but also perennially relevant and universally significant—these are qualities characteristic of a classic work of art, qualities bearing the indelible signature of a master craftsman. Because Achebe's works have been able to cast their spell on readers all the world over for more than thirty years, he has gained recognition, in India and elsewhere, as Africa's leading literary guru, an enchanter and sage whose words carry extra weight. And because his popular following continues to grow year by year, he will surely remain a guru—perhaps India's only African guru—for many years to come.

A CHECKLIST OF INDIAN SCHOLARSHIP ON ACHEBE

Bernth Lindfors and Bala Kothandaraman

Ali, Ahmed. "Some Reflections on the Novel." *Journal of Indian Writing in English* 17.1 (1989): 1-11.

Asnani, Shyam M. "Quest for Identity Theme in Three Commonwealth Novels." *Alien Voice: Perspectives on Commonwealth Literature*. Ed. Avadhesh K. Srivastava. Lucknow: Print House, 1981; Atlantic Highlands, NJ: Humanities Press, 1982. 128-36.

Birje-Patil, J. "*Kanthapura* from an African Perspective." *Commonwealth Literature: Problems of Response*. Ed. C.D. Narasimhaiah. Madras: Macmillan, 1981.102-6.

Chandar, K. M. "Colonialism and Literature: A Study of Some Indian and African Novelists in Their Social Context." Diss. U of Mysore, 1981.

Dheram, Prema Kumari. "Cultural Nationalism in the Novels of Chinua Achebe and Ralph Ellison." Diss. Osmania U, 1987.

Elias, Mohamed. "Time in Achebe's 'Girls at War': Presence of Nigerian Past." *Commonwealth Quaterly* 2.6 (1978): 17-23.

Gowda, H.H. Anniah. "Achebe's *Things Fall Apart* and Ahmed Ali's *Twilight in Delhi*." *Literary Half-Yearly* 21.1. (1980): 11-18; rpt. in *Commonwealth Fiction*. Ed. R.K. Dhawan. New Delhi: Classical Publishing Co., 1988. Vol. 3. 41-49.

----. "The Colonial Encounter: Achebe's Criticism." *Literary Half-Yearly* 22.2 (1981): 17-22.

Guha, Naresh. "The Design of a Novel from Africa." *Jadavpur Journal of Comparative Literature* 16-17 (1978-79): 26-37.

Gupta, Balarama G.S. "Chinua Achebe's *Things Fall Apart*: A Few First Responses." *Literary Endeavour* 1.2 (1979): 55-61.

Iyengar, K.R. Srinivasa. "Commonwealth Literature: Themes and Their Variations." *National Identity: Papers Delivered at the Commonwealth Literature Conference. University of Queensland. Brisbane, 9th-15th August, 1968*. Ed. K.L. Goodwin. London and Melbourne: Heinemann, 1970. 18-32.

JanMohamed, Abdul Rahman. "The Politics of Literary Generation in the African Colonial Situation: An Examination of the Works of Joyce Cary, Isak Dinesen, Chinua Achebe and Ngugi wa Thiong'o." Diss. Brandeis U, 1976.

——. "Chinua Achebe: Colonial Situation and the Generation of Realism." *Jadavpur Journal of Comparative Literature* 18-19 (1980-81): 31-59.

——. *Manichean Aesthetics: The Politics of Literature in Colonial Africa.* Amherst: U of Massachusetts Press, 1983.

——. "Sophisticated Primitivism: The Syncretism of Oral and Literate Modes in Achebe's *Things Fall Apart.*" *Ariel* 15.4 (1984): 19-39.

Joneja, Om Prakash, "Colonial Consciousness in Recent Black American, Indian and African Fiction with Special Reference to the Novels of Richard Wright, Ralph Ellison, James Baldwin, Raja Rao, R.K. Narayan, Mulk Raj Anand, Chinua Achebe, T.M. Aluko and James Ngugi." Diss. Maharaja Sayajirao U of Baroda, 1981.

Jussawalla, Feroza and Reed Way Dasenbrock. Eds. *Interviews with Writers of the Postcolonial World.* U Press of Mississippi. Forthcoming.

Kar, Prafulla C. "The Image of the Vanishing African in Chinua Achebe's Novels." *The Colonial and the Neo-Colonial Encounters in Commonwealth Literature.* Ed. H.H. Anniah Gowda. Mysore: The Director, Prasaranga, U of Mysore, 1983. 149-59.

Katamble, V.D. "*Kanthapura* and *Things Fall Apart:* Two Sthalapuranas." *Littcrit* 12.1-2. (1968): 65-78.

Khan, A.G. "Achebe's *Things Fall Apart* and *No Longer at Ease.*" *Indian PEN* 46.2 (1984): 11-15.

Khayyoom, S.A. "The Neo-Anthropological Novels of Chinua Achebe." *Commonwealth Fiction.* Ed. R.K. Dhawan. New Delhi: Classical Publishing Co., 1988. Vol. 3. 24-40.

——. "The Tragic Pattern in the Novels of Chinua Achebe." *Commonwealth Quarterly* 36 (1988): 49-54.

Kirpal, Viney. "*Things Fall Apart:* A Colonial Novel." *Literary Endeavour* 4.1-2 (1982): 33-38.

——. "Fiction of the 'Third World' in English." *ACLALS Bulletin* 6.1

(1982): 76-88.

----. *The Third World Novel of Expatriation: A Study of Emigre Fiction by Indian, West African and Caribbean Writers.* New Delhi: Sterling, 1989.

----. "The Third World Fiction." *Commonwealth Fiction.* Ed. R.K. Dhawan. New Delhi: Classical Publishing Co., 1988. Vol. 3. 210-25.

Kothandaraman, Bala. "'Where This Rain Began to Fall. . .': A Reading of *Arrow of God.*" *Osmania Journal of English Studies* 17 (1981): 73-81.

----. "'Okoli's Death: A Pointer towards the Narrative Design of Chinua Achebe's *Things Fall Apart*'--Another View." *Journal of Literary Studies* 4.2 (1981): 77-84.

----. "The Sense of Order in Selected Novels of Chinua Achebe, V.S. Naipaul and R.K. Narayan." Diss. Osmania U, 1984.

----. "A Note on the Passage of Ogbazulobodo in Achebe's *Arrow of God.*" *ACLALS Bulletin* 7.6 (1986): 48-53.

----. "'When a Man Fails Alone': Okonkwo's Death in *Things Fall Apart.*" *Osmania Journal of English Studies* 23-24 (1987-88): 119-27.

Krishnamurthy, Sarala. "A Stylistic Analysis of the Fictional Works of Chinua Achebe and Ngugi wa Thiong'o." Diss. Bangalore U, 1989.

Mallikarjuna Rao, P. "*No Longer at Ease*: A Note on the African Writing." *Kakatiya Journal of English Studies* 7 (1985-86): 73-81.

Maria, Jessy. "The Image of the Emerging Individual in West African Fiction." M.Litt. thesis. Central Institute of English and Foreign Languages, Hyderabad, 1981.

Nahal, Chaman. "Conformity and Protest in Nigerian and Kenyan Fiction." *The New Literatures in English.* New Delhi: Allied Publishers, 1985. 152-70.

Nandakumar, Prema. "Chinua Achebe." *The Glory and the Good: Essays on Literature.* Bombay, London, and New York: Asia Publishing House, 1965. 285-304.

----. "The Theme of Religion in the Fiction of Chinua Achebe." *Journal of the Karnatak University: Humanities* 20 (1976): 257-64.

Narajagannadh, B.V. "Individual and Society in the Novels of Chinua

Achebe." Diss. Nagarjuna U, 1985.

Narasimhaiah, C.D. "Where Angels fear to tread: Chinua Achebe and Wole Soyinka as Critics of the African Scene." *Literary Criterion.* 23.1-2 (1988): 222-36. Spl. issue on African Lit.

Nazareth, Peter. "Out of Darkness: Conrad and Other Third World Writers." *Conradiana* 14 (1982): 173-87.

Pal, Dipak. "Okoli's Death: A Pointer towards the Narrative Design of Chinua Achebe's *Things Fall Apart.*" 3.1 (1980): 29-38.

Paniker, K. Ayyappa. "Man and God in Indian and African Fiction: A Study Based on *Kanthapura*, *Arrow of God*, and *Mookajji's Visions.*" *Commonwealth Literature: Problems of Response.* Ed. C.D. Narasimhaiah. Bombay, Calcutta, Delhi: Macmillan India, 1981. 107-16.

Parameswaran, Uma. "Amid the Alien Corn: Biculturalism and the Challenge of Commonwealth Literary Criticism." *World Literature Written in English* 21 (1982): 240-54.

Parasuram, A.N. *Minerva Guide to Chinua Achebe: NO LONGER AT EASE.* Madras: Minerva Publishing House, 1971.

----. *Minerva Guide to Chinua Achebe: THINGS FALL APART.* Madras: Minerva Publishing House, 1975.

Patnaik, Eira. "Proverbs as Cosmic Truth and Chinua Achebe's *No Longer at Ease.*" *Africana Journal* 13. 1-4 (1982): 98-103.

Purushothaman, N. "Social Vision in the Novels of Chinua Achebe." M.A. thesis. Bharathidasan U, 1985.

Rai, Jagdish. "The Wounded Psyche of Africa as Reflected in Achebe's *Arrow of God*, Plomer's *Turbott Wolfe* and Ngugi's *River Between.*" *Recent Commonwealth Literature.* Ed. R.K. Dhawan, P.V. Dhamija and A.K. Shrivastava. New Delhi: Prestige Books, 1989. Vol. 2. 116-29.

Rajab, Ahmed. "Achebe's Land." *Africa Events* February 1985, p. 54.

Ramamurti, K.S. "Patterns of Distinctiveness in the Language of Commonwealth Fiction: A Comparative Study of the Language of Achebe, Naipaul, Narayan and Nagarajan." *Literary Half-Yearly* 22.2 (1981): 85-100.

Ramakrishnan, E.V. "The Novel of Memory and the Third World Reality: Gabriel Marquez and Chinua Achebe." *Colonial Consciousness in Commonwealth Literature: Essays Presented to Professor C.D.Narasimhaiah.* Ed. G.S. Amur and S.K. Desai. Bombay, Madras, New Delhi: Somaiya Publications,

1984. 124-31. Rep. *Indian Readings in Commonwealth Literature*. Ed. G.S. Amur, V.R.N. Prasad, et al. New Delhi: Sterling Publishers, 1985. 124-31.

Rao, A Ramakrishna. "The Politics of Anglophone African Discourse." *Indian Response to African Literature*. Eds. A Ramakrishna Rao and C.R. Visweswara Rao. New Delhi: Prestige, 1992 (forthcoming).

Rao, Meera. "A Study of 'Realism' in the Novels of Selected African and Indian Writers: Achebe and Ngugi, Anand and Markandaya." M.Litt. thesis. Central Institute of English and Foreign Languages, Hyderabad, 1980.

Rao, P. Bhargavi. "The Use of Myth in Contemporary African Literature." Diss. Osmania U, 1988

Roy, Anjali, "African Oral Traditions and the Nigerian Novelist: A Study of Chinua Achebe, Wole Soyinka, Amos Tutuola." Diss. IIT, Bombay, 1988.

Roy, Anjali. and Viney Kirpal. "African Oral Traditions and the Nigerian Novelist: Chinua Achebe." *ACLALS Bulletin* 7.6 (1986): 77-96.

----. "English Words, Ibo Lives: A Study of Language in Achebe's Novels." *Commonwealth Fiction*. Ed. R.K. Dhawan. New Delhi: Classical Publishing Co., 1988. Vol. 3. 50-60

Shahane, V.A. "*Things Fall Apart*: Achebe's Craft of Fiction." *Scholar Critic* 1.1 (Jan 1981): 34-39.

Shankar, D.A. "Chinua Achebe as Critic: A Note." *The Colonial and the Neo-Colonial Encounters in Commonwealth Literature*. Ed. H.H. Anniah Gowda. Mysore: The Director, Prasaranga, The U of Mysore, 1983. 229-34.

Sharma, S.K. "Okonkwo and his *Chi*: Notes towards a mythological approach towards Achebe's Novels." *Indian Response to African Literature*. Eds. A. Ramakrishna Rao and C.R. Visweswara Rao. New Delhi: Prestige, 1992 (forthcoming).

Sharma, T.R.S. "Chinua Achebe and V.S. Naipaul: One Version and Two Postures on Postcolonial Societies." *The Colonial and the Neo-Colonial Encounters in Commonweallth Literatures*. Ed. H.H. Anniah Gowda. Mysore: Prasaranga, The U of Mysore, 1983. 83-94.

Shirwadkar, K.R. "Faith and Frustration in Third World Consciousness." *Indian PEN* 46.2 (1984): 4-10.

Shivanath. "An Introduction to Black African Literature." *Indian Literature* 25.1 (1982): 5-26.

Singh, Satyanarayan. "Chinua Achebe and the Dynamics of Change in African Sensibility." *Indian Journal of English Studies* 25 (1985): 49-57.

——. "Achebe's Social Vision in *Arrow of God*." *The Colonial and the Neo-Colonial Encounters in Commonwealth Literatures*. Ed. H.H. Anniah Gowda. Mysore: Prasaranga, The U of Mysore, 1983. 121-34.

Sinha, A.K. "The Common Concerns." *Africa Quarterly* 23.3-4 (1983): 65-86.

——. "Chinua Achebe's *Things Fall Apart*: The African Point of View." *Explorer*. 2 (July 1991): 11-18.

Sivaramakrishnan, V. "Chinua Achebe: Progenitor of a Literary Tradition." *Triveni* 56.2 (1987): 45-54.

Sridhar, S.N. "Non-Native English Literatures: Context and Relevance." *The Other Tongue: English Across Cultures*. Ed. Braj B. Kachru. Oxford and New York: Pergamon Press, 1982. 291-306.

Sundaram, Geeta. "Chinua Achebe: A Critical Assessment of his Novels." M.Phil. thesis. Osmania U, 1983.

Tejani, Bahadur. "Culture versus Literature." *Writers in East Africa*. Ed. Andrew Gurr and Angus Calder. Nairobi, Kampala, Dar es Salaam: East African Literature Bureau, 1974. 131-49.

Tripathi, Prayag D. "*A Man of the People:* A European Aesthetic?" *Ngoma* 1.1 (1981): 36-54.

Urs, S.N. Vikramraj. "*Things Fall Apart*: A Novel from the 'Dark' Continent." *Commonwealth Quarterly* 1.1 (1976): 28-34.

Vijayasree, C. "The Impact of Colonialism on Commonwealth Fiction: A Study with Reference to Achebe, Anand and Lamming." Diss. Osmania U, 1986.

——. [Ravichandra]. "A Journey Through History: A Study of Chinua Achebe's Fiction." *Commonwealth Fiction*. Ed. R.K. Dhawan. New Delhi: Classical Publishing Co, 1988. Vol. 3. 226-37.

Visweswariah, H.S. "Black Orpheus Unveiled: A Note on African Writing in English." *Triveni* 45.4 (1977): 16-19.

Vyas, Bhanushanker Odhavji. *Untenanted Skies: Glimpses of the Ethnic Universalism in V.S. Naipaul and Chinua Achebe*. South Harrow: Ruchirkala, 1984.

Waghmere, J.M. "Chinua Achebe's Vision of the Crumbling Past." *Indian Readings in Commonwealth Literature*. Ed. G.S.Amur, V.L. Prasad, et al. New Delhi: Sterling Publishers, 1985. 117-23.

WORKS CITED

Achebe, Chinua. *Things Fall Apart*. London: Heinemann, 1958.

----. *No Longer at Ease*. London: Heinemann, 1960.

----. *Arrow of God*. 1964. London: Heinemann, 1975.

----. *A Man of the People*. London: Heinemann, 1966.

----. "The Black Writer's Burden." *Presence Africaine* 31.59 (1966): 135-40.

----. *Girls at War and Other Stories*. London: Heinemann Educational Books, 1972.

----. "The Role of the Writer in a New Nation." *African Writers on African Writing*. Ed. G.D. Killam. London: Heinemann, 1973. 7-13.

----. *Morning Yet on Creation Day*. London: Heinemann Educational Books, 1975.

----. "An Image of Africa." *Massachusetts Review* 18 (1977): 782-94.

----. *The Trouble with Nigeria*. London: Heinemann, 1983.

----. *Anthills of the Savannah*. London: Heinemann, 1987.

----. *Hopes and Impediments: Selected Essays 1965-1987*. London: Heinemann, 1988.

Acuna, Rodolfo. *Occupied America: The Chicano's Struggle Toward Liberation*. San Francisco: Canfield, 1972.

Agovi, Kofi E. *Novels of Social Change*. Tema, Ghana: Ghana Publishing Corp., 1988.

Althusser, Louis. *Lenin and Philosophy and Other Essays*. Trans. Ben Brewster. London: NLB, 1971.

Anozie, Sunday O. "Negritude, Structuralism, Deconstruction." Gates 105-25.

Appiah, Anthony. "Strictures on Structures: The Prospects for a Structuralist Poetics of African Fiction." Gates 127-50.

Arasanayagam, Jean. *Trial by Terror*. Hamilton, New Zealand: Rimu Books, 1987.

Arnold, Matthew. *Culture and Anarchy*. 1869. Cambridge: Cambridge

UP, 1960.

Ashcroft, Bill, Gareth Griffiths, and Helen Tiffin. *The Empire Writes Back: Theory and Practice in Post-Colonial Literatures*. London: Routledge, 1989.

Barthold, Bonnie Jo. "Three West African Novelists: Chinua Achebe, Wole Soyinka and Ayi Kwei Armah." Diss. U Arizona, 1975.

Bell, Bernard. *The Afro-American Novel and Its Tradition*. Amherst: U of Massachusetts P, 1985.

Bergson, Henri. "Laughter." *Comedy*. Ed. Wylie Sypher. Garden City, NY: Doubleday Anchor, 1956. 61-190.

Berlin, Isaiah. *Karl Marx: His Life and Environment*. 1948. 4th ed. Oxford, London and New York: Oxford UP, 1978.

Blamires, Harry, ed. *A Guide to Twentieth Century Literature in English*. London: Methuen, 1983.

Bottomore, Tom, ed. *Karl Marx*. Englewood Cliffs, NJ: Prentice-Hall, 1973.

Brennan, Timothy. *Salman Rushdie and the Third World: Myths of a Nation*. New York: St. Martin's Press, 1989.

Brodber, Erna. *Myal*. London and Port of Spain: New Beacon Books, 1988.

Brownjohn, Alan. "Redeeming the Time: Recent Novels." *Encounter* 70 (April 1988): 57-61.

Brydon, Diana. "New Approaches to the New Literatures in English." *Westerly* 34.3 (1989): 23-30.

Burke, Edmund. *Reflections on the Revolution in France*. 1790. Harmondsworth: Penguin, 1984.

Carroll, David. *Chinua Achebe*. 1970. 2nd ed. London and Basingstoke: Macmillan; New York: St. Martin's P, 1980.

Chametzky, Jules, ed. *Black Writers Redefine the Struggle: A Tribute to James Baldwin*. Amherst: Institute for Advanced Study in the Humanities, 1989.

Chandrasekera, Ruchira. "The Thing Lies There." Unpublished ms.

Cook, David. *African Literature: A Critical View*. London: Longman, 1977.

Chinweizu. "An Interview with Chinua Achebe." *Okike* 20 (1981): 19-32.

Davidson, Jim. "Interview: Chinua Achebe." *Meanjin Quarterly* 39.1 (1980): 35-47.

de Grandsaigne, J. and S. Nnumonu, eds. *African Short Stories in*

English: An Anthology. London and Basingstoke: Macmillan, 1985.

Dharker, Rani. "An Interview with Salman Rushdie." *New Quest* 42 (1983): 351-60.

Disraeli, Benjamin. *Sybil: or The Two Nations*. 1845. London: Oxford UP, 1969.

Eagleton, Terry. *Criticism and Ideology: A Study in Marxist Literary Theory*. London: Verso, 1976.

Egudu, R.N. "Achebe and the Igbo Narrative Tradition." *Research in African Literatures* 12.1 (1981): 43-54.

Eko, Ebele. "The Novels of Achebe in English and American Reviews." Unpublished paper presented at the Symposium for Chinua Achebe's Sixtieth Birthday held at the University of Nigeria, Nsukka, 12-14 Feb. 1990.

Emenyonu, Ernest, and Pat Emenyonu. "Achebe: Accountable to Our Society." *Africa Report* 17.5 (1972): 21-27.

Ephraums, Wilhelm. "Promenade in August." *Navasilu* 7/8 (1987): 39.

Etherton, Michael. *The Development of African Drama*. London: Hutchinson, 1982.

Fanon, Frantz. *The Wretched of the Earth*. Trans. Constance Farrington. New York: Grove, 1966.

----. *Black Skin, White Masks*. Trans. Charles Lam Markmann. New York: Grove, 1967.

Ferdinando, Shamindra. "The Week." *The Island* 25 Feb. 1990.

Fernando, Basil. "Yet Another Incident in July 1983." *Evelyn My First Friend and Other Poems*. Wattala, Colombo: N. Fernando, 1985. 12-13.

Fernando, Siromi. "Style Range in Sri Lankan English Fiction: An Analysis of Four Texts." *World Englishes* 8.2 (1989): 119-31.

Finnegan, Ruth. *Oral Literature in Africa*. Oxford: Clarendon, 1970.

Gates, Henry Louis, Jr., ed. *Black Literature and Literary Theory*. London and New York: Methuen, 1984.

Gordimer, Nadine. "A Tyranny of Clowns." *New York Times Book Review* 21 Feb. 1988: 1, 26.

Graham-Yooll, Andrew, quoted in *Literature Matters*, 4 (April 1990): 3-5.

Granqvist, Raoul. "The Reception of Achebe in Sweden." Unpublished paper presented at the Symposium for Chinua Achebe's Sixtieth Birthday held at the University of Nigeria, Nsukka, 12-14

February 1990.

Griffiths, Gareth. "Language and Action in the Novels of Chinua Achebe." *African Literature Today* 5 (1971): 88-105.

----. "Being there, being There: Postmodernism and Post-Colonialism: Kosinsky and Malouf." *Ariel* 20.4 (1989): 132-47.

Gunatilleke, Godfrey. "A Language Without Metaphor." *Community* 1.2 (1954): 55-69.

Gupta, Balarama G.S. "Chinua Achebe's *Things Fall Apart*: A Few First Responses." *Literary Endeavour* 1.2 (1979): 55-61.

Harlow, Barbara. *Resistance Literature*. New York: Methuen, 1987.

Hutcheon, Linda. "Circling the Downspout of Empire: Post-Colonialism and Postmodernism." *Ariel* 20.4 (1989): 149-75.

Innes, C.L. *Chinua Achebe*. Cambridge: Cambridge UP, 1990.

----. "The Story of this Country: Language, Discourse and Power in *Anthills of the Savannah*." Unpublished paper presented at the Symposium for Chinua Achebe's Sixtieth Birthday held at the University of Nigeria, Nsukka, 12-14 Feb. 1990.

Irele, Abiola. "The Tragic Conflict in Achebe's Novels." *Black Orpheus* 17 (1965): 24-32.

Izevbaye, D.S. "Nigeria." *Literature of the World in English*. Ed. Bruce King. London: Routledge and Kegan Paul, 1974, 136-53.

JanMohamed, Abdul R. *Manichean Aesthetics: The Politics of Literature in Colonial Africa*. Amherst: U of Massachusetts P, 1983.

Jayawickrema, Wipul. "From Here to Eternity." Unpublished ms.

Jeffares, A.N. "The Study of Commonwealth Writing." *Journal of the Royal Society of Arts* 117 (1968): 16-30.

Jeyifo, Biodun, ed. *Contemporary Nigerian Literature: A Retrospective and Prospective Exploration*. Lagos: Nigeria Magazine, 1985.

Katrak, Ketu H. "Decolonizing Culture: Toward a Theory of Postcolonial Women's Texts." *Modern Fiction Studies* 35 (1989): 157-79.

Killam, G.D. *The Writings of Chinua Achebe*. London: Heinemann, 1977. Revised ed.

Kolakowski, Leszek. *Main Currents of Marxism: Its Rise, Growth and Dissolution*. Vol. 1. New York: Oxford UP, 1978.

Lamming, George. *Natives of My Person*. London: Longman Caribbean, 1972.

Larson, Charles. *The Emergence of African Fiction*. Bloomington and

London: Indiana UP, 1971.

Lessing, Doris. *The Golden Notebook*. New York: Simon and Schuster, 1962.

Lindfors, Bernth. "The Palm-Oil with which Achebe's Words are Eaten." *African Literature Today* 1 (1968): 3-17.

----, Ian Munro, Richard Priebe, and Reinhard Sander, eds. "Interview with Chinua Achebe." *Palaver: Interviews with Five African Writers in Texas*. Austin: African and Afro-American Research Institute, University of Texas 1972. 5-12.

Lohafer, Susan. *Coming to Terms with the Short Story*. Baton Rouge and London: Louisiana State UP, 1983.

----, and Jo Ellen Clarey, eds. *Short Story Theory at the Crossroads*. Baton Rouge and London: Louisiana State UP, 1989.

Macaulay, T.B. "Minute on English Education in India." Rpt. in Uma Parameswaran. *A Study of Representative Indo-English Novelists*. New Delhi: Vikas, 1976, 3.

Marable, Manning. *African and Caribbean Politics: From Kwame Nkrumah to the Grenada Revolution*. London: Verso, 1987.

Marcus, James. "Tyrant's Gambit." *The Nation* 16 April 1988: 540-41.

May, Charles E. ed. *Short Story Theories*. Athens, Ohio: Ohio UP, 1976.

McCartney, Barney Charles. "The Traditional Satiric Method and Matter of Wole Soyinka and Chinua Achebe." Diss. U Texas at Austin, 1976.

Modern Fiction Studies. 28.1 (Spring 1982) Special Number on "The Modern Short Story."

Moss, Robert. "Writing and Politics." *West Africa* 11 August 1986: 1676-77.

Narayan, R.K. *Swami and Friends*. 1935. Mysore: Indian Thought Publications, 1988.

----. *The Guide*. 1958. Mysore: Indian Thought Publications, 1975.

Nazareth, Peter. "Out of Darkness: Conrad and Other Third World Writers." *Conradiana* 14 (1982): 173-87.

Ngugi wa Thiong'o. *Homecoming: Essays on African and Caribbean Literature, Culture and Politics*. London: Heinemann, 1972.

----. *Writers in Politics: Essays*. London: Heinemann, 1981.

----. *Detained: A Writer's Prison Diary*. London: Heinemann, 1981.

----. *Decolonising the Mind: The Politics of Language in African Literature*. London: James Currey, 1986.

Nnolim, C.E. "The Form and Function of the Folk Tradition in Achebe's Novels." *Ariel* 14.1 (Jan. 1983): 35-47.

Ogungbesan, Kolawole. "Politics and the African Writer." *African Studies Review* 17 (1974): 43-53.

Ong, Walter J. *Orality and Literacy: The Technologizing of the Word.* London and New York: Methuen, 1982.

Pieterse, Cosmo, and Dennis Duerden, eds. *African Writers Talking: A Collection of Radio Interviews.* London: Heinemann Educational Books; New York: African Publishing Corp., 1972.

Podis, Leonard A., and Yakubu Saaka. "Achebe's *Anthills of the Savannah* and Ngugi's *Petals of Blood:* The Creation of a Usable Past." Unpublished ms.

Pryce-Jones, David. "Links to Bruised Hearts." *Times Literary Supplement* 9 Oct. 1987: 1106.

Rajan, Balachandra. "Identity and Nationality." *Commonwealth Literature: Unity and Diversity in a Common Culture.* Ed. John Press. London: Heinemann, 1965. 106-9.

Rambukwelle, P.B. *The Desert Makers.* Colombo: n.p., 1985.

Ravenscroft, Arthur. "African Literature V: Novels of Disillusion." *Journal of Commonwealth Literature* 6 (1969): 120-37.

Reid, Ian. *The Short Story.* London and New York: Methuen, 1977 (*The Critical Idiom* series).

----. "Destabilizing Frames for Story." Lohafer and Clarey: 298-310.

Roscoe, Adrian A. *Mother is Gold: A Study in West African Literature.* Cambridge: Cambridge UP, 1971.

Rutherford, Anna. "Chinua Achebe: Interview." *Kunapipi* 9.2 (1987): 1-7.

Said, Edward W. *Orientalism.* New York: Random House, 1979.

----. "Intellectuals in a Post-Colonial World." *Salmagundi* 70-71 (1986): 44-64.

----. "Through Gringo Eyes: With Conrad in Latin America." *Harper's Magazine* April 1988: 70-72.

----. "Goodbye to Mahfouz." *London Review of Books* 8 December 1988: 10-11.

Schleh, Eugene P.A. "Chinua Achebe: Voice of Africa." *Essays in Arts and Sciences* 12.2 (1983): 125-34.

Seneviratne, Maureen. "Mirage." *Navasilu* 7/8 (1987): 61-63.

Soyinka, Wole. *The Interpreters.* London: Andre Deutsch, 1965.

----. *Myth. Literature and the African World.* Cambridge: Cambridge

UP, 1976.
----. *Death and the King's Horseman*. London: Methuen, 1982.
----. *A Play of Giants*. London and New York: Methuen, 1984.
----. "The Critic and Society: Barthes, Leftocracy and Other Mythologies." Gates 27-57.
----. *Six Plays*. London and New York: Methuen, 1984.
Taiwo, Oladele. *Culture and the Nigerian Novel*. London: Macmillan; New York: St. Martin's P, 1976.
Tiffin, Helen. "Post-Colonialism, Post-Modernism and the Rehabilitation of Post-Colonial History." *Journal of Commonwealth Literature* 23.1 (1988): 169-81.
Updike, John. "Books: In Dispraise of Powers That Be." *New Yorker* 13 June 1988: 114-16.
vanden Driesen, Cynthia. "From Rogue to Redeemer: R.K. Narayan's *The Guide*." *International Fiction Review* 6.2 (1979): 166-70.
Wajesinha, Rajiva. *Acts of Faith*. New Delhi: Navrang, 1985.
Wijeratne, Kamala. "A House Divided." *A House Divided*. Ambatenna, Sri Lanka: n.p., 1985. 8.
Wilson, R.R. "Slip Page: Angela Carter, In/Out/In the Postmodern Nexus." *Ariel* 20.4 (1989): 96-133.
Wren, Robert M. *Achebe's World: The Historical and Cultural Context of the Novels*. Harlow: Longman, 1981.
Yerima, Ahmed. "Cutting across Classifications: Achebe as a Postmodernist Writer." Unpublished paper presented at the Symposium for Chinua Achebe's Sixtieth Birthday held at the University of Nigeria, Nsukka, 12-14 Feb. 1990.

CONTRIBUTORS

Cynthia vanden Driesen teaches Australian, English and Postcolonial literatures at the University of Perth, W. Australia.

Radhamani Gopalakrishnan teaches in the English Department at the Sri Venkateswara University, Tirupati, India.

Dhruba Gupta teaches History at the University of Calcutta.

Ashley Halpé teaches in the English Department at the University of Peradiniya, Sri Lanka.

Feroza Jussawalla is an Associate Professor of English and Director of Honours Programme at the University of Texas at El Paso.

Viney Kirpal teaches in the Department of Humanities and Social Sciences at the Indian Institute of Technology, Bombay.

Bala Kothandaraman teaches in the English Department at the Osmania University, Hyderabad.

Bernth Lindfors teaches English and African Literatures at the University of Texas at Austin.

Supriya Nair is a postgraduate student in the English Department at the University of Texas at Austin.

Anuradha Dingwaney Needham is an Assistant Professor of English at Oberlin College, Ohio.

Charles Ponnuthurai Sarvan teaches in the English Department at the University of Bahrain.

Govind Narain Sharma teaches British, Indian-English and African literatures at Acadia University in Nova Scotia, Canada

Kirpal Singh teaches English at Nanyang Technological University, Singapore.

INDEX